Leading Systemic School Improvement Series

...helping change leaders transform entire school systems

This ScarecrowEducation series provides change leaders in school districts with a collection of books written by prominent authors with an interest in creating and sustaining whole-district school improvement. It features young, relatively unpublished authors with brilliant ideas, as well as authors who are cross-disciplinary thinkers.

Whether an author is prominent or relatively unpublished, the key criterion for a book's inclusion in this series is that it must address an aspect of creating and sustaining systemic school improvement. For example, books from members of the business world, developmental psychology, and organizational development are good candidates as long as they focus on creating and sustaining whole-system change in school district settings; books about building-level curriculum reform, instructional methodologies, and team communication, although interesting and helpful, are not appropriate for the series unless they discuss how these ideas can be used to create whole-district improvement.

Sin   rting books aren't
inc   actice — in other
wc   d language. Ide-
all   ow to create and
sus   categories:

                                                                       rtant. This is
the   ic school im-
pro   ow systemic
sch   the driving
for   provement
car

                                                                     what. Pos-
sib   s scaled up
to   rformance
sch   arning and
lea   ile enough
to r

                                                                  how. Pos-
sib   ol systems;
too   ng systemic
cha   ss and out-
con   vement.
                                                             4-9800 or

fmc

Leading Systemic School Improvement Series
Edited by Francis M. Duffy

1. Francis M. Duffy. *Moving Upward Together: Creating Strategic Alignment to Sustain Systemic School Improvement*. 2004.
2. Agnes Gilman Case. *How to Get the Most Reform for Your Reform Money*. 2004.

How to Get the Most Reform for Your Reform Money

Agnes Gilman Case

Leading Systemic School Improvement Series, No. 2

ScarecrowEducation
Lanham, Maryland • Toronto • Oxford
2004

Published in the United States of America
by ScarecrowEducation
An imprint of The Rowman & Littlefield Publishing Group, Inc.
4501 Forbes Boulevard, Suite 200, Lanham, Maryland 20706
www.scarecroweducation.com

PO Box 317
Oxford
OX2 9RU, UK

British Library Cataloguing in Publication Information Available

Library of Congress Cataloging-in-Publication Data

Case, Agnes Gilman, 1950–
  How to get the most reform for your reform money / Agnes Gilman Case.
    p. cm. — (Leading systemic school improvement series ; no. 2)
  Includes bibliographical references and index.
  ISBN 1-57886-148-9 (pbk. : alk. paper)
  1. Education—United States—Finance. 2. Educational change—United
States. I. Title. II. Leading systemic school improvement ; no. 2.
LB2825.C324 2004
371.2'06—dc22

                                            2004002676

⊗™ The paper used in this publication meets the minimum requirements of
American National Standard for Information Sciences—Permanence of
Paper for Printed Library Materials, ANSI/NISO Z39.48-1992.
Manufactured in the United States of America.

Contents

Tables

Introduction

It has been two decades since *A Nation at Risk* was published, but what has happened in education because of that publishing? Has anything changed? Is our nation educationally less at risk than it was? Is educational reform any closer? Are students achieving at a higher level when compared to other industrialized nations? What progress has been made toward the stated goal of a world-class education for all students? In the day-to-day operations in a school district, is education being delivered to students in a demonstrably different way than before, or do classrooms look the same as they did twenty years ago? This is the real proof of reform. It is not the passionate speeches, not the flowery words, not the best of intent, but the differences in delivery of education that create increased achievement for students.

The existing system of traditional public education is now in a fight for its very existence. Charter schools, private schools, cyber schools, homeschooling, parochial schools, school vouchers, and school choice have all developed as attempts to provide better education by providing an alternative to the public schools. And all of these alternative forms of schools are occurring because *nothing has substantively changed in public education*. It is imperative that this lack of progress be addressed.

So who is responsible for leading this necessary change? The federal government produced *A Nation at Risk*, so it would be reasonable to expect that the federal government should be leading the charge to remove that risk from our nation; however, that has not proved to be the case. State and federal governmental agencies do not have a very good track record in assisting those professionals "in the trenches" to reform education; the words have been lofty and the vision has been moving, but laws have been passed with little or no money attached to them. Technical guidance from the government (the creators of the laws) to help educators understand the laws has been late in coming, sometimes after the deadlines for implementation of those very laws. Advice from the government has been inconsistent. Many times, a question asked on Monday will have a different answer from a different person on Tuesday or Wednesday. Sometimes when an educator calls a telephone number listed for assistance, the people answering the phones are not able to offer any help at all. There has, however, been a marked increase in paperwork.

In the stated interest of local control, the federal government has assigned responsibility for the implementation of these laws to the individual states. The states, in their turn, have passed that responsibility down to the individual districts, and where the federal government has not provided money for the implementation, the states do not provide funds either. One might expect or hope that guidance from the states, being more local than the federal government, might be more specific. This has not been shown to be so. Guidance from the states has also frequently been lacking, or has been contradictory to federal guidance. The denouement of all this political and educational drama is that school districts have laws and regulations with short implementation timelines, with little assistance, with no additional money to meet the requirements, yet with all of the responsibility to produce outcomes.

This is the situation that now exists. The district stands alone on the firing line as the primary implementer of a myriad of laws and regulations to improve education, without help from those who have created and passed the laws. The superintendent and the board of education in every district are accountable for complying with these regulations *and* producing the results mandated by law. How can a district succeed at this task? That is what this series is about—the district and its role in reforming education. This particular book in the series is not a book for accountants, school district business administrators, or treasurers. This is a book for the educator who has not been trained in educational finance and who wants to understand this issue more deeply. This book will provide the change leader with two very necessary things: the vocabulary necessary to talk about the financing of reform, and guidance regarding how to ensure that the maximum amount of money is secured for reform.

Nearly everyone agrees that schools are not producing the type of students that this society and this country need. (But some research has shown that when people are asked about schools, they will say that their own district is doing fine, but those "other" schools need help.) No matter what reform is sought, however, it always comes back to one essential question: How does a district pay for this reform? To further complicate this question, the financing of reform cannot be separated from the other questions of reform: new programs, different configurations of schools, new curricula, updated methods of teaching, and so on. Since all of the areas of reform are linked, the reader will find information on financing that includes ideas from other areas.

New programs may need new materials, or additional training for teachers and staff. More staff and different staff may be required, or technology may have to be included. Buildings may require modification or redesign. Whether or not a reform can be implemented completely or partially, or the level of effectiveness of a reform, oftentimes hinges on the level of funding available, the source of that funding, and how that funding is used. Educational reform is not primarily about money; it is about the students. However, no longer can an administrator say, "I don't deal with the money," or "Money is not important in education." An astute educator needs to know about money and how to use it in order to help any reform come about.

There is a common catch phrase that sounds trite, and many educators endorse this phrase and use this phrase in speeches and communications, yet there are fewer educators who actually implement it. It is one of those truisms that are much easier to say than to do: *Change leaders need to "think outside the box."* Most change leaders will have noticed through their own years in education that one of the hardest things for an educator to do, much more so for a whole system, is to change. They will all have heard, numerous times, the objection "But we've always done it that way!" Teachers have lived through open classrooms, team teaching, multiage classrooms, whole language, phonics, SRA reading, old math, new math, teacher-proof materials, teaching as a science, and teaching as an art, to name but a few of the past educational movements. All of these programs and philosophies have come and gone. Some teachers embraced the programs whole-heartedly and implemented them, only to find lack of support, so they returned to methods that they knew. Others simply continued doing things in the way they deemed best. After a few years (sometimes after even one year) the latest idea in education was replaced with another. Now those of us at the district level need to acknowledge that we did our share in this, supporting first one program, then another, in a kind of educational schizophrenia. Nonetheless, teachers kept on teaching and, to the credit of those teachers, students continued to learn to read, write, and do math. Did the students learn as much as they should have? Did they learn the skills that they needed to prepare for the twenty-first century? That is the conundrum that our profession is currently striving to address.

Change leaders have to approach the beliefs and practices in education with an open mind. In education there are firmly entrenched ideas that have been passed from generation to generation. These are ideas that were revolutionary in their time. In fact, the very idea of a free, public education, now the standard, was once considered shockingly innovative. American culture and the world have changed, for good or for ill, from that "Little House on the Prairie" version of society and education, and even from the social order of fifty or twenty years ago. No longer are there air-raid drills because the relationship of super-powers has changed. Instead there are "lock-down drills" for intruders or bomb scares.

This is a world culture of communication. Information on every aspect of life is readily available and relentlessly examined. Patients visiting a doctor's office no longer take any utterance from a physician as gospel truth; they search the Internet and get a second or third opinion. Fewer people rely solely on "experts" or the conventional wisdom. By its actions the culture embraces the belief that unexamined ideas will cause stagnation and be deleterious to the quality of life. This same relentless examination of ideas should be applied to education. All areas of education must be assessed with a critical eye, not with the intent to assign blame, but with the intent to make education better. It is not productive to look back, but only to look forward. Education as a profession must answer the question "How can educators be even more effective in doing what educators do, that is, in bringing knowledge to children?"

The financing of educational reform is only one of those areas that demand that change leaders think differently. State and federal funding formulas that were designed to prevent deviation from "traditional" schooling by manipulation of funding may currently limit the implementation of that evolutionary thinking. However, these existing formulas can be used more effectively. In the meantime groups and individuals need to lobby against these archaic rules. A change in funding rules will allow not only thinking about financing reform in a nontraditional way but also the application of that thinking. Existing moneys will be able to be used in a different way.

There are a number of areas of finance that can be used for the support of educational reform. This book will discuss those major areas in eight chapters. Chapter 1 will discuss the basic attributes that the change leader must exhibit in order to be able to spend money effectively, those being the attributes that create and maintain public trust. Without these attributes any financial work can be questioned and mistrusted, but the spending of money in a different way will be even more difficult. Chapter 2 will refer to state funding, with its myriad formulas; what data points are important to track; and what questions the change leader should ask the school district business administrator. Chapter 3 will move on to federal funding, with the new regulations of No Child Left Behind, again including issues of data and questions to ask. These chapters address the governmental issues of funding reform over which the change leader will have a minimum of control.

There are some sources of funding, however, over which the change leader will have more control. Chapter 4 deals with taxes, for example. Taxes are the "hot button" issue in every community, and yet they are one of the main sources for financing education. Taxes are also an area where districts are able to have a greater degree of control than over the larger governmental sources. Competitive grants are another source of financing and can be from various sources. Grants have very strict rules usually for both funding and compliance, as will be seen in chapter 5 as well as in chapter 3. Chapter 6 will discuss the smaller and more local ways of financing reform, like partnerships and foundations. This is an area where the individual districts can become very creative and specialized based on community needs.

For each of these funding sources, chapters 2 through 6 will explain what a district can and cannot do, or should and should not do, in using these funding sources. While no one can have all of the answers in regard to funding educational reform, it is hoped that this book will be able to share ideas with its readers, and to stimulate that "outside-the-box" thinking as it applies to each individual district and its own set of circumstances.

Chapter 7 brings up a very controversial concept. Since a change leader must be able to think "outside the box," all ideas must be considered in the quest to provide reform for the students. This chapter will discuss the concept of using charter schools to assist the change leader in bringing about that reform.

This book will continue with a chapter on what we need to do as educators going forward. It is not enough to just identify a problem, no matter how well one can talk about it. One must also offer possible solutions and actions to remediate the problem. One of the favorite slogans in the 1960s and 1970s was "If you're not a part of the solution, you're a part of the problem." This is a truism in education. The educator who clings to old methods of delivering education—even though those methods have worked for years and even though he or she does not actively resist changing—becomes part of the problem we are facing. The passive but recalcitrant educator becomes just one more factor that can be an obstacle to change.

Following chapter 8 is a list of the resources I consulted while writing this book and forming the philosophies it contains, as well as additional resources for the change leader. I have consulted actual practitioners of educational finance to provide information for the change leader. These are the professionals who work with these issues every day, but, on occasion, reference will be made to various reading material. Just as it is valuable to learn from the research, it is equally valuable to learn from the people who are immersed in the practical, day-to-day application of knowledge. I provide a bibliography of the literature and the practitioners I consulted so that the reader may seek more detail, if desired.

Because numbers and finance are a cause for anxiety for many educators, I have made a concerted effort to ensure that this book is usable, practical, and "user-friendly." As little financial jargon as possible is used except where necessary for issues of clarity. In that case, the term is explained for the reader.

Before proceeding to the next chapter I want to make it very clear that I am a passionate advocate of public education. Education is the only way to secure our national and personal liberties and to allow everyone to meet his or her personal goals. It is the only way to ensure equity for all and to preserve peace. I have been a teacher, and I have been an administrator, but I will always consider myself a teacher and be proud of that fact. In my view, teaching is the highest calling that a person can have: to pass on learning to the next generation. The work a doctor does is very important and may determine life or death, but the work that a teacher does can determine the quality, or lack of it, of not only the life of a student, but also the impact of that life on the larger society. Education is so important! Nonetheless, in a spirit of self-discovery, introspection, and total honesty, all who aspire to be change leaders are obligated to look at the part that educators have played and still play in the problems that we face today. A change leader cannot control governments, boards of education, parents, the media, or community members. The change leader *can*, however, control his or her own actions and beliefs. In fact, that is all that the change leader *can* control. It is more profitable, therefore, for the change leader to look at what he or she *is* able to control rather than railing about what other constituencies should do. Self-knowledge is imperative.

It is also imperative that the change leader broaden his or her concept of the term "funding" of educational reform. The most common way of thinking about funding is to simply acquire more money, a task that is not as easy to do as to say. The purpose of this book is to show that seeking additional funds is only one way to identify money that can be applied to reform. An alternative process that the change leader may choose to use is to ensure that the existing money is used to its maximum potential by making those existing moneys "work smarter." The goal in either case is to make available the maximum amount of funds because the more money that is available, the greater is the opportunity for the change leader to use that money for reform. If this book can in any way help change leaders to think differently about financing reform, then it will have achieved its purpose.

CHAPTER 1

Financing Reform Is More Than Just Spending the Money

Simply having and spending money is not the only important aspect of funding educational reform. Equally as important is how the use of that money is directed. The money for reform must be spent to increase achievement in a meaningful way by setting a focus on the programs and methods that are successful. Money must be spent in a way to increase the public trust in schools and the confidence that education can succeed. The philosophies that are the underpinning of these beliefs about education and reform are probably the hardest things to learn and the most difficult things to change.

As noted in the introduction to this book, it is important for the change leader to not limit his or her knowledge, influence, and power by ignoring the financial areas of educational reform. Change leaders can cite educators who seem to be proud that they do not understand, nor do they wish to understand, financial issues. They give the impression that dealing with financial issues is a "dirty" subject; one that is not raised in polite educational company. These same people will tell you that their concern is only with the curriculum and with the students because those things are at the core of education, and they choose to deal only with those important things. Change leaders know that the students are the most important concern in education, but there is a great deal more to consider when one is seeking district change.

By failing to address all of the relevant issues, the change leader does a disservice to the students he or she desires to serve. If a district is going to reform education for the students, then the change leaders should prepare to go about this change in the most effective way. The change leader will be most effective when he or she has an idea of all of the aspects that will affect a reform, and finance is one of those areas. After all, the very best curriculum cannot be implemented, and the greatest amount of concern for the students can have little or no impact on reform if there are not sufficient funds to enact the reform with maximum efficacy.

In this book, the term "funding" will not refer solely to the act of acquiring cash money to fund reform. Rather, the concept of funding will include maximization of existing resources and reallocation of resources as additional "funding" or support options for the change leader.

Before any money at all is actually spent on an educational reform there is one seminal question that needs to be asked, and answered: Whom will this reform benefit? Of course all educators will say that it is the students, but is that what actions reveal? The change leader must consider questions such as the following: Does the money go directly to the classroom or is it used for other purposes? Is the money that was applied for or received with the goal of reform used to fund existing programs that are not relevant to the reform? Is the money used for building alterations or technology that is not applicable to the reform you want to implement? Do the teachers get the materials and training needed to implement the reform? If truthful answers reflect anything other than the benefit of the students as a first and foremost priority, the self-questioning must continue. A school district cannot afford to operate with any agenda other than the benefit to the students when reforming education.

In order to facilitate reform, the primary goal of a change leader must be to establish trust within the school community. If the community does not trust what is said, how can the district expect to institute a change? There are a few very basic attributes that the change leader must exhibit in order to be able to effectively establish and maintain this trust in order to make change in a district and implement reform. These five attributes belong to an era of our history when "spin doctors" did not exist; when everyone knew "what the definition of *is* is"; and when lawyers were used for wills, house closings, and divorces rather than to file suit because a fast-food purveyor's hot coffee was too hot. As the first attribute, an effective change leader has to have integrity, both personally and professionally. The second quality is accountability. It goes without saying that fiscal accountability is a must in establishing trust, but the district will need to demonstrate educational accountability also. Third, the change leader needs to have a focus. Nothing can be accomplished without a goal. Fourth, the change leader's style of governance has to include decentralized decision making within the district; he or she has to be willing to give up total control of the reform and not become ego-involved. For the fifth and final attribute, as the leader of reform one must COMMUNICATE, COMMUNICATE, and COMMUNICATE again!

None of these attributes is optional, nor is one more important than the others. To build and maintain the trust necessary to support reform, *all* of these qualities must be present in the change leader. The greater the degree to which he or she exhibits these qualities, the greater will be the chance of succeeding at making change.

TRUST

Right now society as a whole is suffering a severe lack of trust in all governmental agencies, and what all educators need to realize is that school districts *are* governmental agencies. Therefore districts suffer from that general sense of mistrust even if there is not specific mistrust. Internally, a school district may be able to intellectually separate itself from the state legislature and the politicians in Washington. To the average member of the public, however, a school district is a part of the larger government of "them." "They" are the sometimes nameless, always amorphous groups of people who wield power over the lives of the rest of the population. You have heard the statements: "They" say that. . . . "They" don't care. . . . "They" never listen. . . . To the people on the streets of the community who do not know us personally, "they" are the elected officials at all levels of government and, yes, "they" are the school district.

WHAT HAPPENED TO THE TRUST?

This lack of trust has always been a part of the growing cynicism about government that started in the 1960s. Citizens have seen presidents go to war even when the country as a whole, and perhaps even the world, was not supportive of that. Baby boomers read carefully and listen closely every time someone brings up the subject of Social Security for fear that this benefit will no longer be available to them as they age, and they have no control over that. Governors, mayors, and other local officials raise taxes, which no one ever likes when it happens. These officials also determine how much property is worth and whether or not a given community is protected adequately with fire and police coverage. And these are only a few of the areas that elected politicians influence, over which "they" have control and the members of the public do not. These politicians and their decisions affect daily life and the quality thereof for all of the constituents in their own political province, yet in many areas no improvement has been seen. Members of the public do not feel that their voice is heard by "them," nor are the public's concerns taken into account. For these reasons and more, much of society does not trust state, federal, or local governments. (Nor do educators trust those governments, if truth be told.) Any governmental organization, large or small, from national to the most parochial, is suspect.

The lack of trust no longer stops with governmental agencies, though. It has expanded to include all societal organizations that have power over large groups of people. Multiple incidents where national and multinational corporations, who are supposed to be working for the shareholders under the guise of capitalism, are failing to follow their own fiduciary responsibility have encouraged and emphasized this mistrust. These corporations are giving huge bonuses to executives while cutting pay or benefits for workers, laying off workers, or even filing for bankruptcy, as some airline companies have done. They are engaging in unethical, immoral, even illegal practices to manipulate the companies for the benefit of a small group of people. This happened in the Enron Corporation. It is no longer possible to have faith in the honesty and integrity of the accountants who are asked to keep watch on other companies, as the Arthur Andersen scandal attests. News articles refer to corporations that have hidden their funds, not revealed financial information, made illegal loans to executives, and created accounting nightmares. It is clear to the public that corporations are not trustworthy, either, even though these public companies are supposed to be accountable to their shareholders through their profit and loss status.

Religious organizations were always held to be honest and working for the good of the people. More and more we are finding cover-ups of wrongdoings perpetrated by the very people who were supposed to be teaching the rest of the population how to be good and moral members of society.

Even the venerable *New York Times* has had problems with stories that are not researched or with use of freelance writers who are not even accredited.

Is it any wonder, then, that people don't trust the schools either? There are people in all communities, regardless of the size of the community, who "know" that the school districts are hiding money; that teachers and administrators do not earn their pay; that taxes are set at a rate higher than is necessary to support education; and so on. Candidates run for positions on the board of education for the specific purpose of finding out what the district is "hiding." Some boards of education want to micromanage districts down to the smallest details because they don't trust district leaders.

There is also the distrust of school districts that springs from the belief, the perception, or perhaps the experience, of realizing that students can graduate from school not knowing how to read or do math at an acceptable level, a level that allows them to hold a job or participate as a citizen. In some cases education, as a profession and an organization, is not even trusted enough to do the job that has been assigned to it, much less make itself over with reforms. Many people, educators included, lament the failure of other professions to remake their own profession. How can doctors discipline other doctors; or lawyers examine other lawyers? Can police review boards looking at charges against other police units make a decision that can be trusted? Should education be exempt from this public doubt? Think of it from the point of view of society at large.

Many times these statements and accusations a mistrusting public makes are not correct, but the perceptions still exist. How does a district combat them? Does the change leader say, "Trust me! I'll spend the money on effective educational reform"? Some districts take this route, but it is a mistake. A school district will have to *prove* its ability to spend the reform money well. Is this unfair to the district? Perhaps it is, but it is unavoidable based on the state of society as it now exists. The effective change leader cannot afford to simply state that something is not true and go on about the business of the district. The leader has to deal with the concerns public questioning raises. He or she has to treat them as valid even if it is believed that they are not.

It is troubling, but there is also a mistrust of school leaders among the staff who work for the selfsame district. Spend time with any school faculty and one will hear stories about principals, superintendents, or directors who are not considered trustworthy even to the staff. Or perhaps it is just that the staff members have heard so many promises that were not realized. To demonstrate this, in the 1980s one school district created an innovative, districtwide reform package. It was a joint creation of the school district and the teachers' union and contained changes in the way that education was structured, changes in the behaviors of the teachers, and, coincidentally, a very large increase in pay for those teachers. Many of the staff members accepted the pay while overtly saying that they would not go along with any of the reforms that were proposed because they didn't believe either the superintendent or the union heads when they said the reforms would make a difference. These were not bad people or bad teachers. They were frustrated and disappointed staff members. The change leaders had not built the credibility that was needed to sustain change. Current change leaders need to prevent this from happening in their own districts. The change leader should apply all of the suggestions for use with community groups to staff members as well.

Demonstration of the following five steps (integrity, accountability, focus, decentralized decision making, and communication) will show constituents and staff that they *can* trust the district to spend public money in a way that will improve education in the schools. These steps will restore the faith of the public, and will prove the trustworthiness of the school district, which is an absolute necessity if a district is to reform education. The district's learning community will be more willing to support the district not only in reform, but also in all other areas of education.

THE STEPS TO ESTABLISHING TRUST

Step 1: Integrity

It is very important that the people in charge of spending the money to finance educational reform be of the highest integrity, not only professionally, but personally as well. Professionally, of course, these people need to be honest to a fault, and must follow all the rules of finance precisely and correctly, not because it is the politically correct thing to do, but because it is the *right* thing to do. Financial decisions must be based on the reform effort and not on personal preferences (extra benefits for certain employees, extra money or support for people the administrator "likes" or who are well-connected politically, for instance). Financial records must be clear and must be open to perusal if someone would like to do that. Reports should be simple, easy to understand, and accurate.

The change leader charged with spending the money must have personal integrity also. In a word, one must be congruent. (This is an important point in literature on business reform that the educational reform movement has not always embraced.) Congruence means simply that the words that the person spending money says and the actions that he or she takes must send the same message. The change leader's behavior will reflect his or her beliefs. Unfortunately, congruence is sorely lacking in many areas of education today and can literally defeat the implementation of a new program or a reform. Change leaders will have seen the lack of congruence in education many times: the administrator who says he or she wants different ideas, but reacts badly when someone actually differs from his or her opinion. Another example that we see is the superintendent who says that the students are most important, but will reduce teacher numbers to provide funds to save an ineffective program. The effective change leader must say what he or she means, and mean what he or she says.

Step 2: Accountability

If there is any area where trust is vital between a district and its public, that area is finance. It seems that whenever there is a scandal involving a school district, the charges in the scandal will almost always include allegations of financial mismanagement of public money. There have been superintendents who have used district funds for their own purposes; there have been district business administrators who have absconded with district moneys; there have been board of education members who have asked for or received kickbacks from vendors in return for granting contracts. Probably every member of the public even marginally interested in education has heard at least one of these stories of misuse of public funds. While it may not be fair, community members extrapolate those possibilities and apply them to their own districts. People ask themselves, or each other, "If it could happen in district XYZ, why couldn't it happen here?" This cynicism is what we have to combat.

In order to fight this lack of trust, a district has to be willing and eager to do the following things to show fiscal accountability, regardless of the source of those funds:

At the beginning of a grant, a fiscal year, or a new program, tell constituencies how the district anticipates spending the money. Naturally the change leader will not be able to identify exactly the number of pencils or books that will be used for the program, but it is possible to give approximate amounts of money and show the proportion of different types of expense. Divide the budget total into estimates for each of the following areas: professional staff (salaries and benefits), support staff (salaries and benefits), equipment, materials and supplies, and services purchased from outside the district. These are the most common areas of expense. For clarity for the community and the staff, the change leader may also wish to divide the equipment category into nontechnology equipment and technology equipment, as well as adding designations for textbooks, travel, and transportation. These last areas are the areas that will garner the greatest number of questions from the public.

At regular intervals during the *fiscal period* (the grant year, fiscal year, or period of duration of a project), report on the status of the finances. Is the budget "on track," meaning that expenses are proceeding as expected? Have there been any dramatic overexpenditures or underexpenditures? What is the prognosis for the remainder of the fiscal period?

At the end of the project, grant, or fiscal year, evaluate the use of the money. Was the budget accurate? Where does next year's budget need modification? What were the outcomes of the program?

A Sample Project Budget

In table 1.1 there is an example of a simple project budget. Note that this project budget does not need to include specific numbers of smaller items. The change leader should work with the district business administrator to create the budget in the format that the district uses, and in a way that aligns with the state budget codes. For simplicity, only one segment of the budget code is used here: the *object code*. These particular object codes are from New York State. The object code tells the type of expenditure the district is making, such as salaries or materials and supplies. Chapter 2 provides more specific information on the language of accounting.

From a proposed initial budget report like this, the community will be able to see in which areas the district anticipates expenses, as well as the estimated cost of the total project. The public will be able to determine the largest areas of expense and the proportion of funds that are spent on each. Because a school district is a "people-intensive" organization, it is expected that the largest part of the expenses in education will be for personnel, but the change leader should also be prepared to share with questioners an idea of what kinds of purchases are included in each expense area or category, for example, How many computers will be purchased with the three thousand dollars in technology equipment? Why is travel included? Whom is it for? Why is there a transportation component? The change leader must have these answers.

The change leader should avoid creating program budgets that have too many *budget lines* (categories of expense) or budget lines with very small amounts of money in them. (A budget line is simply a budget code with a description and an amount of money, as one can see in table 1.1.) An example of too much specificity would be a budget with a

Table 1.1. Proposed Project Budget with Money Allocated by Category

Object Code	Description	Budgeted Amount
15	Professional Staff	$220,000.00
16	Support Staff	$25,000.00
20	Equipment (Nontechnology)	$2,000.00
22	Equipment (Technology)	$3,000.00
40	Purchased Services	$11,000.00
40	Transportation	$5,000.00
45	Supplies and Materials	$2,000.00
45	Textbooks	$1,500.00
46	Travel	$1,500.00
80	Benefits	$66,100.00
	Project Total	**$337,100.00**

Note: Amounts are for example only and do not reflect an existing budget.

budget line for office paper, a budget line for construction paper, and a budget line for copy paper. Another example would be budget lines that carried amounts of fifteen or twenty dollars. The school district business office will assist the change leader in developing this budget.

Along the way, change leaders should give regular and clearly stated financial updates. All of the educational constituencies will want to see how the project is progressing fiscally. The usual timeline for financial reporting is once monthly.

Table 1.2 expands the original project budget into an example of an interim report for the project budget that might be seen approximately one quarter of the way through the project timeline. About one fourth of the salaries and benefits have been spent, which is appropriate at this juncture. Most of the money for equipment, supplies, and textbooks has been spent, which is also logical because in the beginning of a project the classes or groups needed for the project are being prepared or established.

The change leader must be sure to monitor the budget at regular intervals. Just as the change leader would be with his or her own checkbook, the change leader must be watchful. If it seems that expenses are going to be higher in one area than was thought, expenses must be lowered in other areas to ensure that the project does not overspend the funds that were allocated to it.

Table 1.2.   Project Budget Interim Report Showing Expense Categories and Amounts Spent to Date

Object Code	Budget Code Description	Amount Budgeted	Amount Spent to Date	Amount Remaining
15	Professional Staff	$220,000.00	$60,179.12	$159,820.88
16	Support Staff	$25,000.00	$6,012.79	$18,987.21
20	Equipment (Nontechnology)	$2,000.00	$1,799.03	$200.97
22	Equipment (Technology)	$3,000.00	$2,973.29	$26.71
40	Purchased Services	$11,000.00	$2,000.00	$9,000.00
40	Transportation	$5,000.00	$179.00	$4,821.00
45	Supplies and Materials	$2,000.00	$1,582.33	$417.67
45	Textbooks	$1,500.00	$1,439.00	$61.00
46	Travel	$1,500.00	$600.00	$900.00
80	Benefits	$66,100.00	$17,049.44	$49,050.56
	Project Total	**$337,100.00**	**$93,814.00**	**$243,286.00**

Note: Amounts are for example only and do not reflect an existing budget.

Finally, upon the completion of the project, or at the end of the grant period or fiscal year, the leader must be able to tell the community exactly where and how the money was spent. This can be done by using the same format as the original budget. Create the final document showing both the original figures and the final ones. In this way the public will be able to see what was intended to be spent as compared to what was actually spent. Nothing about the finances is hidden here and fiscal accountability is clear.

Table 1.3 expands on the original project budget to show an example of a final budget report. This is where the change leader may need to defend expenditures in relation to the project outcomes. He or she will need to know the program well and be able to explain discrepancies between the original budget and the final budget report. The willingness to do this and to be open with the community will establish and ensure credibility. This is also where some educators get nervous. Nonetheless, if numbers are accurate and the change leader is truthful, then even if members of the public disagree, they will not be able to accuse the district of mismanagement or manipulation. In presenting this final report, the change leader should never allow himself or herself to become defensive. The public is questioning the use of public money. If the leader seems defensive, the public may perceive him or her as hiding something or being guilt-ridden. This is counterproductive in building that public trust.

Table 1.3 has a column that shows the difference between expenses that were proposed originally and what was actually spent. The numbers in this column that are in parentheses indicate that more was spent than was proposed (negative balance). The positive numbers in this column show that money was left in these budget lines (also referred to as *budget codes*); not all of the money allocated to these was spent. The overriding concern is the project total line. This line (the "bottom line") should never be in parentheses (negative or "in the red") without justification.

In table 1.3, what the public will immediately note is that the project has been completed within budget. This is important to the community. It shows that the school district is spending taxpayers' money well, not frivolously. Salaries and benefits cost a little more than anticipated, but most other expenses were less.

Table 1.3.   Final Project Budget Report Showing Final Expenses and Variances

Object Code	Budget Code Description	Amount Budgeted	Final Expenses	Variance (Difference)
15	Professional Staff	$220,000.00	$223,447.19	$(3,447.19)
16	Support Staff	$25,000.00	$24,775.41	$224.59
20	Equipment (Nontechnology)	$2,000.00	$1,810.97	$189.03
20	Equipment (Technology)	$3,000.00	$2,973.29	$26.71
40	Purchased Services	$11,000.00	$10,000.00	$1,000.00
40	Transportation	$5,000.00	$2,673.00	$2,327.00
45	Supplies and Materials	$2,000.00	$2,001.85	$(1.85)
45	Textbooks	$1,500.00	$1,483.66	$16.34
46	Travel	$1,500.00	$1,460.00	$40.00
80	Benefits	$66,100.00	$66,435.71	$(335.71)
	Project Total	**$337,100.00**	**$337,061.08**	**$38.92**

Note: Amounts are for example only and do not reflect an existing budget.

It should be noted that only very rarely do the initial budget numbers and the final budget numbers match exactly. That would be an unrealistic expectation. If this is what the district's community expects, however, it is incumbent upon the change leader to educate that community.

Put simply, the change leader needs to articulate a financial plan, follow that financial plan, and evaluate it regularly and rigorously.

Educational Accountability

At the end of a fiscal year, project, or grant year, the change leader must then evaluate the use of the money in the budget through evaluation of the educational outcomes of the project (for the purposes of this book it is assumed that the project relates to the district reform that has been designated). For each time period (fiscal year, grant year, etc.), the district must be willing to show that the money spent on educational reform has been spent effectively to bring about changes in the district. The change leader must present data, even if it is anecdotal at first, that demonstrates that the use of the reform has caused a different outcome. Hard data, of course, frequently will rely on scoring of assessments and other conditions that will not be as immediate as the financial data. Start with the anecdotal and report the hard data as soon as it is available. Remember that a culture exists where the media has promulgated the expectation that every problem can be handled in a thirty- or sixty-minute block of time. The community wants rapid answers, so the change leader will need to be as timely as possible in presenting information.

There is one incredibly important point to remember when it comes to the question of accountability: *Questions from the public are not a bad thing.* Members of the public are trying to understand where the money has gone. They want to see results. Public education is financed with public funds, much, if not all, of it coming from local pockets in one way or another. People have a right to expect an accounting. Our culture demands results and explanations. Step 5 will talk about communication in greater depth. The change leader must remember that a school district is a *public organization*, supported by *public money*. Therefore, the school district needs to be accountable for how that money is spent.

Step 3: Focus

Focus is the effective and directed use of the money allocated to reform. Focus is something that some districts may not have, not because of ill-conceived plans, but because of human nature. In a school district the number of different programs grows over the years. New thinking or new regulations bring new classes and programs, yet once a given program is established many school districts are loath to discontinue that program. Some districts try to pursue organized abandonment of programs, by evaluating results and narrowing down district programs to the ones that work best. In many instances in school districts, though, little or no abandonment occurs. Instead a political negotiation takes place irrespective of data showing programs' success or lack of it.

The change leader will recognize the behaviors that may occur. There may be a program or programs that have been in place for twenty years, so they have become "tradition." No one wants to cut this kind of program because of the outcry of the traditionalists: "We've always had this program!" Administrators start negotiating with the superintendent or board to protect programs that they hold dear without the hard data to support them. Staff members call in all of the favors that they have done for other staff members. The change leader will have heard negotiations such as "Remember when I supported your guidance program? Well, now I want you to support my summer program."

Those who are successful will keep their programs. Those who are not will lose theirs. All of this is done without regard to program results. The staff becomes divided and morale declines. The change leader and the district must not fall into this trap!

Instead, set the criteria for a successful program. These criteria need to be objective and clear and rely on data. If a program does not meet the criteria do not be afraid to let it go. The public will understand if a program is not showing results and you remove it from the district, but if the public sees a program that is ineffective (or that they perceive as ineffective) continuing to receive funding the district will lose that public trust that it has been trying so hard to build. If the program is ineffective, let it go. If it is only perceived as such, show data as to how and why that program is having the desired results. The money for education is limited, and it is the public's money. It must be spent in a way that is as effective and as directly connected to reform as possible.

Establishing the Focus

To ensure that money is well spent, and spent only on programs that are effective for reform, the district needs to take three important steps in providing the focus:

First, perform a thorough needs assessment of the district. Don't rely on community perceptions or even only on the perceptions of the change leader for this assessment. Ask for data and use it. What reform is needed? Probably, more than one area of weakness will be indicated, but do not try to challenge every deficiency at once. Prioritize the district's needs and search for the *power reform*, the change that will have the farthest-reaching effects on the district and the students. Is it a code of conduct? Is it the manner in which subjects are being taught? Is it reading skills? Is it math? Is it teacher expectations? Is it administrative expectations? Is it structure or organization? Is it assessments? Is it the curriculum? Look at everything.

Second, the district should make a conscious choice of which reform the district is going to be supporting. Too often school districts "back into" reforms: the district may decide that since the state is saying a program or reform is important, the district should try it; or perhaps the XYZ corporation is giving grants for technology, so the district applies for the money thinking that it will decide how to use the money after it arrives. This is not the way to determine which reform to support. Use the data, make the choice, and let everyone in the learning community know what that choice is.

Third, identify programs that have proved successful in demonstrating that reform and showing that the reform has brought about, in a similar district, the educational change that the district seeks. Just because something has been successful in the district next door, or has succeeded in a district that your district hopes to emulate, do not assume that every district will necessarily show the same results from the same programs. Each learning community is different in terms of expectations, demographics, resources, and so on; that is why it is so important to know your community well.

Reform for the sake of reform is futile and frustrating. It becomes a public relations piece or simply window dressing, not real reform. Direct the money that supports educational reforms to those programs that are effective. Do not spend the reform money on "this would be nice" programs. Do not spend the reform money on programs that have "always been there." Do not spend the reform money on programs that are the "babies" of certain people. Funds are limited. So is time. The need and desire to reform is urgent. The change leader and the district must spend effort and resources on what works best.

Step 4: Decentralized Decision Making

Throughout the writings on business reform, books and consultants all tout the wisdom of team management. Translated into educational parlance, this means that the superintendent gathers around himself or herself a team of individuals with different skills. This team is the group that gathers data, performs the needs assessment, looks at the results of that assessment, and chooses the path to reform. When building this management team, the worst thing a superintendent can do is gather a group of only those people who think the same way that he or she does about issues. Reform involves doing things differently in education and thinking about things differently. The management team has to have individuals with different ideas. It needs change agents and mavericks, but it also needs traditionalists. The differences in ideas, perceptions, knowledge, and experience can create a synergy that brings new ideas to the table and stimulates creative thinking if allowed to do so.

Business research also supports the idea that the person closest to the implementation of a decision be given decision-making power. The idea in education is to give the individual school sites more autonomy over choosing what they need, when they need it, and how to use it. It is easy to find examples of centralized decision making: the superintendent who decides what reading text will be used without consulting the reading teachers or specialists, or who hires teachers without input from the principals with whom the teachers will be working; or the business administrator who tells the schools how much each can spend on equipment without regard to what may be needed. Hopefully these examples have become passé. The effective change leader will share his or her power to decide.

Decentralizing Finances

In financing a reform, the financial responsibilities are also shared in an effort to allow the staff at an individual site to make the decisions about how to use the money allocated to it. To allocate reform money, the change leader begins with that project budget in table 1.1, then allocates the reform money to each site where the reform is going to be implemented, but not, however, in isolation. The principals of the buildings need to be involved. The needs and/or desires of each individual site have to be considered. Perhaps one school will need reconstruction, but another will not. One school may need new technology to support the reform. The change leader has to look at each site's allocations based on site needs, then look at the district overall and make sure that district needs are met. Table 1.4 shows a sample allocation of the money in the project budget first introduced in table 1.1.

Table 1.4 includes the *location code* to indicate to which school or project site that money has been allocated. In this example there are two sites where the reform program is being implemented: School A and School B. School A has been assigned the location code *01* and School B has been designated *02*. A *00* location code shows that the expense will be monitored by the district. The length of the total budget has expanded, but the total monetary amount of the project has not.

Table 1.4. Building Project Budget Allocation Showing Division of Allocations by Building

Object Code	Location Code	Budget Code Description	Budgeted Amount
15	00	Professional Staff	$220,000.00
16	00	Support Staff	$25,000.00
20	01	Equipment (Nontechnology)	$1,000.00
20	02	Equipment (Nontechnology)	$1,000.00
20	01	Equipment (Technology)	$2,000.00
20	02	Equipment (Technology)	$1,000.00
40	01	Purchased Services	$6,000.00
40	02	Purchased Services	$5,000.00
40	01	Transportation	$2,500.00
40	02	Transportation	$2,500.00
45	01	Supplies and Materials	$1,000.00
45	02	Supplies and Materials	$1,000.00
45	01	Textbooks	$1,000.00
45	02	Textbooks	$500.00
46	01	Travel	$750.00
46	02	Travel	$750.00
80	00	Benefits	$66,100.00
		Project Total	**$337,100.00**

Note: Amounts are for example only and do not reflect an existing budget.

School A and School B can now have their own smaller budgets specific to each individual site.

Of course, a budget that gives the site-based allocations for the total project is too cumbersome for use at the individual sites. For that reason, the project budget can be broken into smaller budgets. The administrator of each project site will have to monitor only his or her small piece of the project, so financing this reform is becoming simpler still for the site administrator.

Table 1.5 sets out the project budget for School A. This is easier to understand than the expanded allocation budget.

Table 1.5. Building Project Budget Allocation for School A Only

Object Code	Location Code	Budget Code Description	Budgeted Amount
20	01	Equipment (Nontechnology)	$1,000.00
20	01	Equipment (Technology)	$2,000.00
40	01	Purchased Services	$6,000.00
40	01	Transportation	$2,500.00
45	01	Supplies and Materials	$1,000.00
45	01	Textbooks	$1,000.00
46	01	Travel	$750.00
		Building Project Total	**$14,250.00**

Note: Amounts are for example only and do not reflect an existing budget.

Table 1.6.   Building Project Budget Allocation for School B Only

Object Code	Location Code	Budget Code Description	Budgeted Amount
20	02	Equipment (Nontechnology)	$1,000.00
20	02	Equipment (Technology)	$1,000.00
40	02	Purchased Services	$5,000.00
40	02	Transportation	$2,500.00
45	02	Supplies and Materials	$1,000.00
45	02	Textbooks	$500.00
46	02	Travel	$750.00
		Building Project Total	**$11,750.00**

Note: Amounts are for example only and do not reflect an existing budget.

Table 1.6 shows the project budget for School B.

Looking at these two budgets together, it is clear that the two sites did not receive equal funding. This is due to input from the different sites. It appears that School A has greater specific needs in implementing this project.

It is obvious, though, that we have not accounted for all of the money in the project. A third budget, table 1.7, tracks the expenses that the district is responsible for monitoring. These are the personnel and benefit expenses.

Broken down into site-based fiscal responsibility, the project budget is even less frightening to those unaccustomed to educational finance. The responsibility for financial administration at each site is only for expenses that the building can control. The district has a responsibility for $311,100 of the project. School A has its own project budget of $14,250 and School B has a project budget of $11,750. Each principal will be responsible for spending and tracking his or her own money for the reform project. The overall project total is still $337,100, however. Interim and final reports for individual school

Table 1.7.   Building Project Budget Allocation for Districtwide Component Only

Object Code	Location Code	Budget Code Description	Budgeted Amount
15	00	Professional Staff	$220,000.00
16	00	Support Staff	$25,000.00
80	00	Benefits	$66,100.00
		Districtwide Project Total	**$311,100.00**

Note: Amounts are for example only and do not reflect an existing budget.

sites can be created in the same way that these reports are created for the project budget as a whole.

Change leaders can support this entrepreneurialism in the schools only within the parameters of the state. There are certain standards to be met, certain assessments that must be used, and certain skills that must be taught before students can continue on to the next grade. No site-based management system can ignore these things. Nonetheless, the decisions on how to meet these state goals should be the district's, and the district should further allow principals and individual schools to determine, within district parameters, how each site will meet its particular site-based goals that relate to the district and state goals.

Step 5: Communication

A few pages ago, it was boldly indicated that questions from the public are not a bad thing. In fact, a change leader should look forward to these questions as an opportunity to understand concerns or the chance to educate the community about the reform. In some cases, though, educators see questions from the public as automatic accusations that the educator is not doing his or her job. This is a defensive overreaction that is not usually appropriate.

Normally the public questions at a board meeting or other public gathering are to procure more information or seek an explanation. The change leader's response should be to answer clearly or, if he or she doesn't know the answer, promise to look into the matter and get back to the community member. This does not mean, however, that the leader should allow either abuse or personal attacks. There are also some questions that are simply not appropriate for a public venue. Questions involving individual students should always be addressed in private. Accusations or questions about individual staff members should be handled with discretion as well. If any of the questions address issues that are personal to the speaker, the leader should invite that speaker to a personal meeting. The leader must not, however, delay such meetings in hopes that the community members will forget. They won't. They will only remember that they were dismissed or put off, and they will interpret this as "they" don't care or "they" don't want to listen. A meeting with an individual should elicit the same responses from the change leader as a public meeting: the change leader should be open, be honest, investigate the problem, and direct the person to the appropriate individual if necessary.

Perhaps the defensiveness of some educators goes back to old childhood memories where no one questioned the teacher. If a student was punished at school, he or she was punished at home when parents found out about it. No one questioned it and the teacher was always right. Society has outgrown that, however. Due to the turmoil of the sixties and the seventies the culture learned (in fact, many of us taught others) that it was acceptable to question authority. We flaunted it. Now we are living with a society that is comfortable in doing so. Therefore, as a district and as change leaders, we have to embrace this development in society.

There is an aphorism that notes, "A little knowledge is a dangerous thing," meaning that a person should not react based on only a small amount of knowledge, but should research for more information. This applies to the public, community members, parents, taxpayers, staff, *and* the change leader. The way to avoid the danger that is "little knowledge" is to seek more knowledge and to provide more knowledge. The change leader should listen to his or her constituencies and then try to find out more information about a problem. One must not rely on the perceptions and information of only one person or even on only the change leader's observations. One must gather more information. When dealing with members of the learning community, give more information, not less. Do not fall into the trap that some educators have encountered: believing that since something is an educational problem, the public wouldn't understand it or, worse, doesn't need to understand it. With more complete knowledge comes more complete understanding.

"Spinning" in Education

The use of the word *spin* as both a verb and a noun and its current connotation in relation to communication needs to be addressed. One of the most damaging things that can happen to the bond of trust between a school district and its public is for the district to be caught in a "spin" of information. In society at large, information "spins" are commonplace; that is probably one reason why public trust is so low. So if the district doesn't "spin," there is no danger in being found out.

On occasion districts and change leaders use the expression "We want to put the correct spin on things." This metaphor comes from baseball, where the spin on the ball that is pitched determines the speed and the trajectory of the ball as it approaches the batter. The pitcher tries to put the spin on the ball that will get the results that the pitcher or the team seeks. In baseball, the pitcher wants the batter to miss so that the team can claim a victory. In daily usage, putting the correct "spin" on things means showing something in only its best light, and in daily actions that may mean ignoring the more negative side of the issue.

The connotation of "spin" in communication, particularly in education, where we are dealing with children, is negative and manipulative. When a district "spins" information in education, the district stresses the information that it wishes the public to be aware of, not necessarily the complete and accurate information. Following is an example of a "spin" in education.

In this example a district's report card from the state government has been released. There are four levels of proficiency for students, with level 4 being the highest and with students at levels 1 and 2 considered to be at risk. Looking at this imaginary report card objectively, there has been no decrease in the number of students at risk as compared to the previous year, yet the district is bound by law to present this information publicly. What is the district to do? One way to "spin" this information is to ensure that the presenter of the information stresses only the positives: for example, "X percent of students in the district score at level 3 and level 4." To continue this good "spin" the presenter gives a great deal of detail about the level 3 and 4 students; the more information the better. Using information that is irrelevant to, or only slightly associated with, the issue at hand will distract from the negative information. It may be demographic breakdowns of levels 3 and 4, or mobility statistics to show the performance of students who have not moved. The presenter can give information about the programs that have produced these proficient achievers or the training that the teachers received to enable them to help students reach these levels. Another good idea for "spinning" information is to have the informational presentation go on as long as possible. Members of the public, unless they are particularly persistent, will "tune out" after a while if the presentation goes on long enough because our culture has a collectively short attention span. The result of all this work to "spin" the information is just what the district desired: educational prestidigitation. Only positive information about the district has been disseminated; no one has heard about the negative. The district looks successful.

Clearly, "spinning" *cannot* be done if a district is to have effective and trustworthy communication with its constituencies. There are, however, some very simple and commonsense actions to take to ensure ease of communication among all groups in the district.

How to Communicate with the School's Public

Listen. This is the most important action a change leader can take in communicating with constituencies. It is much more important than the talking phase of communication. Before explaining the reform, before sharing that information openly and honestly, even before deciding what reform to pursue, a change leader must listen. And listening is not done only at public meetings. Listening is done every minute of every day to every person encountered. People want to express their needs, their desires, and their concerns, particularly in education, where their children are concerned. Parents and community members want to be heard; they want to be validated and acknowledged. They want someone in power to realize that their point of view has value. The effective change leader will perform this service for others in the role of advocate of educational reform. Additionally, the change leader must not argue or try to impart information unless asked. (This is a classic failing of educators. Educators seem born to give information to others.) One should just listen, ask questions, and expand one's own knowledge. If the change leader can do that for the district's public it will help the process of trust building move forward.

Talk. Be sure to communicate with all relevant constituencies, and even with the constituencies that don't seem relevant. The change leader must talk with parents, PTAs, teachers, staff, neighbors, tax PAC groups, retirees, legislators, politicians, and businesspeople. And he or she must not forget to talk to the students! If anyone knows the schools well it is the children who are the real customers and who spend their days on the receiving end of education and of our reform! One should visit the Rotary Club, the chamber of commerce, the Lions Club, Kiwanis, churches, and service organizations, and talk to anyone who will stand still long enough to listen. The change leader must bring the message of reform to all people in a clear and concise way. The more people who are aware of the goal of reform, the better it is for the schools and the district. When the change leader is willing to talk with others, that will often create the opportunity to listen, also, to the group to whom one is talking. The leader must not squander the opportunity.

Be open and honest. All information needs to be clear and understandable. Any district needs to be open and accessible in sharing information, but this is particularly important for a district that is seeking to do things differently.

An effective change leader cannot use educational jargon. Most people don't understand it; perhaps even some educators don't. When a change leader uses educational jargon it appears elitist, as if the leader were holding himself or herself above everyone else, or even obfuscating a matter. He or she may appear to be intellectually arrogant. The change leader cannot afford to appear as if he or she subscribed to the theory "If you can't dazzle 'em with brilliance, then baffle 'em with bull." If an educational term must be used, it must be explained clearly.

When the change leader explains something, the KISS principle must be used: Keep It Simple, Stupid. He or she should learn to explain terms like "rubric," "gestalt," "annual yearly progress," or other terms common in educational use in simple and clear language. The danger is in making these explanations so simple that it appears that the leader is condescending or talking down to people. While this may seem a very fine line for the change leader to walk, it is well worth the effort.

The change leader must not evade answers. That makes it seems as if he or she were trying to hide something, which is a very bad impression to make with constituencies. If the leader does not know an answer, he or she must say so. It is perfectly acceptable for the change leader to *not* know everything off the top of his or her head. One can look up information to ascertain its accuracy and respond to the person who has the concern or question at a later date. If the change leader is not able to give an answer (if it concerns a contract, a legal matter, or some other information that the leader is bound by law to keep confidential), he or she should say so. The answer "no" with an explanation is more accepted than a garbled, indeterminate answer that sounds abstruse or unsure.

All constituencies must be told what the goal is for the reform that is planned. The school district is spending public money to finance the reform, so the public deserves to know what the goal is. In addition, the community should be aware of the plan to reach that goal. The change leader must tell constituencies about possible pitfalls that the district may encounter on the way to that goal, also. One never wants the public or the board of education to be surprised when something that could have been foreseen goes wrong. There may be benchmarks that the community can look for along the way. As an example, perhaps a goal for prekindergarten students may be that by the end of three months these students will be able to recite the alphabet, and by the end of six months they will be able to write it. The change leaders and the constituencies will be able to judge the effectiveness of the program. People like to know how a program is progressing. Just as in the purely financial area, the district must give regular reports on how the reform is progressing. Even if the district issues a report to say that there is no new information, at least people will remain aware of the topic.

It is true that research shows that when asked, most people will say that their local schools are fine and that it is other schools that need help. A change leader must not make the mistake of relying on that research. As more and more "report cards" are published about the schools, and more and more data is available to compare schools, more and more parents and community members are now asking questions. A community may be satisfied with its middle school, for instance. But what happens when that school appears on a list of schools needing improvement? I have seen very few parents who will dispute that. Instead, they begin to look for the "why" of how the school made the list.

If there is bad news to share, do it honestly. Tell constituents what happened and what is planned to fix the problem. Don't try to "spin" the information so that it looks like the district was totally innocent, or the change leader was totally innocent, or that there is only a silver lining, not a cloud. Community members will not believe it anyway, and the trust that has been built will erode without that honesty.

Do not, however, confuse "open and honest" communication with permission to be unkind in communicating. Honesty is not an excuse to hurt people.

It is necessary to make every effort to find less threatening ways to communicate to the public. Formal board meetings or community presentations may not be the areas where many members of the community are comfortable presenting concerns or asking questions. One might have small, informal "coffee klatches" with the help of parent groups or schools. A smaller group of people can make it easier for others to talk. Having teas or small meetings where community members are invited is another idea. Participation in these invitational meetings should not be limited to those who hold power in the community. The "regular" people, the people who send their children to school but think they have no voice, must be invited, too. The change leader must give them a voice. Community members who think that they have a voice and will be listened to will not show up at board meetings with petitions nor write nasty editorials to the local papers.

As an example of how very important communication is, the change leader should keep in mind a superintendent in one district who changed the athletic team mascot from a stylized Native American because the superintendent felt that it was the right thing to do, but without the required communication between the district and the community. The board membership changed drastically the very next year with very negative consequences for the district, all because of a lack of investment in the time to listen to, and to communicate with, the district's constituencies. Even when the change leader does something for all the right reasons, but has not communicated properly, there can be disastrous effects.

"THINK OUTSIDE THE BOX"

The reader may be thinking now that all of the suggestions in this chapter are already a part of everyday work in education; that they are not "thinking outside the box." If one believes this, that is because he or she already uses these techniques in his or her profession. If a district already has a secure focus, and complete integrity and accountability, and communicates well with all groups, then effective implementation and financing of reform will occur very successfully. To the eternal disappointment of educational reformers everywhere, however, the suggestions in this chapter *are* "thinking outside the box" for too many educators. Scores of educators are totally invested in maintaining the status quo in education. They have become consummate politicians (in the negative sense) in that meeting their own agendas is more important than meeting the agenda of reform and the needs of the students.

This is a sad assessment of a part of the profession, since there are so many who wish wholeheartedly to make a difference for the students. But this is the view of educators and education that many of the members of the public see; the view that many staff members see. In order to address reform a change leader needs to address his or her own beliefs and actions also.

SUMMARY

The primary duty of change leaders is to build trust with all constituencies. It is a sad fact that trust in all governmental entities is lacking, and until that trust exists no reform is going to be as successful as it ought to be, or as successful as the students deserve. There are five steps that the change leader can take, five behaviors that the change leader must demonstrate to build that trust.

First, the people who are actually charged with spending the money in the district have to have consummate integrity.

The second behavior is accountability to the public and to staff in both fiscal and educational areas. Nowhere else can the district lose trust as fast as when there is the least question in the area of finances. No one can afford to be less than proper when dealing with public money. Equally as important is showing that the programs that have been supported have produced positive results for the students. The change leader has to have a plan, follow that plan, and evaluate that plan in order to show both fiscal and educational accountability.

Third, the reform has to have focus. The district needs to concentrate its attention and its efforts on the reform at hand. Otherwise, the district can get a sloppy, piecemeal, or less than effective implementation.

To use behavior number 4, decentralized decision making, the change leader cannot afford to keep all of the managerial authority within himself or herself. He or she has to share power and decision-making authority with other people who are working on the reform. This will result in greater ownership of the program and the process and therefore better implementation.

The fifth and final requirement for building the trust necessary to successfully finance reform is: COMMUNICATE, COMMUNICATE, COMMUNICATE! There is no such thing as too much communication.

The change leader should note that these five steps are not discrete activities, but behaviors that intertwine one with the other. It is the use of these behaviors as a whole that will build the trust that is sought.

Through all of these efforts to build trust, the change leader must "think outside the box" in terms of educational ideas. It is folly to continue to perform the same actions, but expect different outcomes, particularly if one is seeking educational reform.

CHAPTER 2

The "State" of Funding for Educational Reform: State Aid

For many school districts, the largest amount of money they receive is from their state government. However, the purpose of this chapter is not to fully explain the ins and outs of state funding for education. Instead, the intent is to provide the change leader with an overall view of how state aid funding works (or fails to) in providing support for education. The chapter will also provide definitions of the various types of aid that may be available from the state and explain the proper and improper uses of these funds. Additionally, this chapter will describe the sets of data that may be important for the district to be able to produce when filing with the state to receive state aid. While the change leader may not be the designated official to do the data collection (that function usually resides in the district offices, many times in the district business office), the change leader needs to know about the type of information needed so that he or she may provide data that is as accurate as possible. Accurate data will result in the school district receiving the maximum amount of aid to which it is entitled. The change leader must work to maximize existing revenue in order to have the maximum amount of money available to be used for educational reform in the district.

WHERE DOES STATE AID MONEY COME FROM?

The money for funding education (and for funding educational reform) in every state comes from the pockets of every person who pays taxes to that state government. Some people may believe that the state support for schools does not cost anything to the citizens in a given locality. That is a fallacy. The state collects taxes from the residents of the state, puts the money into the state's own coffers, and then divides the available money among school districts according to a set of legislatively determined criteria.

The state legislature will decide how much money will go to educational funding in a given budget year. The amount is based on negotiations between the governor and power groups within the state government. There is frequently a great deal of competition and contradictory information regarding expected revenues and long-term forecasts. While legislators are fighting over education funding they are also looking for funding for all of the other programs that the state supports. Those could be state police funding or staffing the government to continue its operation. All are valid concerns and valuable programs, but how much money each program receives is subject to negotiation.

Once the gross amount of money that will be given to education is determined, legislators must decide which programs to fund within the broader sphere of education and to what level to fund each smaller program. How much funding will go to vocational education? To elementary education? To prekindergarten? There will be lobbying among legislators. Groups from the public lobby every year to have their own selected programs funded. Or these groups may want a proposed cut of a program abandoned. There follows another period of negotiation and compromise.

From this protracted period of negotiating and compromise, school district funding formulas are created and modified. Due to the act of negotiation, these funding formulas often reflect the criteria established by members of the state's legislature rather than the interest of the students. Also, because a political process, rather than objective criteria, determines the formulas, subtle changes in formulas can direct money to particular types of districts or a particular district. So the state aid funding formulas are not based on the need of the students, but on the success of the lobbying efforts.

When it comes to issues of state aid funding formulas, the most effective action that the change leader can take, at this point in time, is to ensure that the school district receives the maximum amount of money possible through the state funding formulas. In order to do that, the change leader must have an understanding of the types of state aid available and know what data is important to track for obtaining the maximum amount of money for the school district.

In an effort to ameliorate some of the abuses of the aid formulas that have developed, some states have added types of *categorical aid* to the funding plan. (Categorical aid may not be spent for any purpose other than what the legislature has directed.) State categorical aid is designed to address the needs of specific programs or types of students that have not, according to the state legislature's assessment, been adequately funded in the regular formulas. Again, since it is a legislative assessment, the process of choosing which programs or students are more deserving of categorical aid is subject to lobbying and influence. The problem with categorical aid for the change leader is that this money may be severely restricted in its use. Also, categorical aid is sometimes a use-it-or-lose-it proposition where the money will return to the state if it is not used by a certain date or on the preestablished types of expenses. The change leader cannot use money given in categorical aid to fund programs that are not approved under that categorical aid. In addition, expenses and compliance must be documented separately from other sources of school district funds.

TYPES OF STATE AID

Each state will have its own panoply of types of state aid. Below are a few of the more common forms. Each state will also have its own individual definitions and processes for application to the state. The school district business administrator should be a great help to the change leader seeking to learn about these issues.

Operating Aid. All states provide general operating aid to each school district at a given level, although the precise title of the aid may differ from state to state. Generally, operating aid can be used for any expense that the school district has legally and ethically incurred: salaries, benefits, debt service, school buses, staff development consultants, and so forth.

Special Education Aid. This is probably the most popular addition to state funding in terms of additional aid. This is at least a tacit admission of the fact that it can be significantly more expensive for a district to educate students with special needs, and to ensure that these students are provided with the same basic education as all other students.

Textbooks. Library Books. Computer Software. Computer Equipment. The funds designated for these purposes are to ensure that all schools have the ability to purchase these items since these items are considered necessary to provide a free and public education.

Vocational Education. This aid is for the classes that provide training in a career: construction, medical technology, computer repair, and so on. Again this recognizes that a course in vocational training will cost more than a mathematics class or English class: each class will serve fewer students because of safety concerns, and the equipment needed to teach this type of class is far more expensive than textbooks and even computers that are used in academic classes.

English as a Second Language. As the number of immigrants to this country increases there is an increasing burden being put on the schools, particularly in the border states. Students who are unable to speak English, or who are deficient in that skill, will require special considerations in order to be educated to the same level as other students. Some states are providing funds for the additional costs of educating these students, but there is still a very public debate occurring over whether or not any state aid should be received for these services. Some assert that the cost of education for these students should be a federal expense, not a local expense.

Capital Aid. It is recognized that the cost of building a new school or renovating an old one can be prohibitive for a school district. Therefore states provide assistance to school districts by granting capital aid based on a formula. This aid may pay for debt interest, debt principal, building renovations, and/or building leases.

Prekindergarten. Some states have recognized the importance of a stress on early literacy and provide funds to support prekindergarten programs.

Tax Relief. In some states the state will provide some additional money if (1) taxpayers in a school district are paying taxes that are deemed to be too high by state criteria, or (2) the district does not have the *tax base* (the assessed value of property) necessary to raise enough money to support education in that district. In this way the yearly increase in taxes can be ameliorated and kept to a minimum level.

Categorical Aid. Categorical aid can be for any purpose the state designates. The difference between categorical aid and other forms of state aid is that the categorical aid *must* be spent on the purpose or program for which the aid was intended. The school district is *not* free to change that usage. Misuse of categorical aid can sometimes result in a loss of that aid. Many times computer equipment and software aid is categorical, as may be those funds for textbooks.

Each state has its own list of types of state aid and of categorical state-aided programs, each with its own set of rules and regulations. The school business administrator for each school district is the staff member who is probably most intimately familiar with these formulas. The change leader should develop a relationship with that staff member and keep the lines of communication open.

THE PARTS OF THE FUNDING FORMULAS

Fortunately or unfortunately, a district cannot change the state funding formulas on its own. In order to maximize the amount of money that is coming to the school district through these formulas, the change leader needs to know the parts of the formulas on which he or she can have an effect. As mentioned earlier in this chapter, the change leader will probably not have the ultimate responsibility for collection of this data. However, the change leader needs to know what data to collect and of which information to be aware. It is difficult to collect data after the fact. It is better to deal proactively with the issue of data collection and make the change leader aware of the information that may be required.

This section of the chapter will define a few of the most common data points, the things that the change leader will want to monitor, or at least be aware of, in order to generate the maximum amount of state aid. Ask the school business administrator which data points are important for your particular program so that you can start accounting for that information from the beginning of the program.

Enrollment. Enrollment is the number of students who are signed up to attend the schools in the district, or to participate in a given program. It is very important that this be an accurate number. If the number of enrollees is too small the district may not receive as much money as it is entitled to from governmental sources. If the number is too large, the state may take back money from the district that the state has already sent and the district has already spent. This is not a good situation for a school district and is guaranteed to cause stress in the business office.

For example, if the change leader's district has an enrollment of one hundred students, the state wants to fund only those one hundred students, no more and no fewer. If the district reports enrollment inaccurately by saying that there are ninety-five students, the state will provide funding for ninety-five students, less than the district needs and less than is appropriate. This money may or may not be recouped from the state at a later date. On the other hand, the district might report enrollment inaccurately by saying that there are 105 students. When other student counts reveal that there are fewer students, the state will ask for the money back, if already given, or simply deduct the money from future payments and send less. Therefore, it is very important for student counts to be as accurate as possible.

Part of that accuracy of reporting is to record the date that a student enters the district *and* the date that a student leaves the district. Usually districts are very good at recording the date of a new student's arrival in a school, but when a child leaves a district, that exit is not always recorded in a timely manner. Different schools within the same district may have different procedures for recording these dates. Some may wait to record the exit until another school district makes a formal request; some may act on a parent's information. The procedure should be the same throughout the district.

Attendance. Attendance is not the same as enrollment, but this is frequently confused. Attendance is the actual number of bodies physically present in each class on a given day or during a given class period. In order to be counted in attendance, the student must also be counted as enrolled. This may seem to be an obvious point, but it isn't. Needless to say, attendance can never be higher than enrollment. As with counting enrollment, a procedure must be established districtwide and followed faithfully. Also, as with the enrollment numbers, it is best to have attendance numbers as accurate as possible, and for the same reasons. Inaccurate attendance numbers can affect the amount of money a district receives.

The change leader may wish to explore the various computer pro-grams that are available for the type of explicit attendance tracking that is beginning to be required.

Weighting. In some states students with special needs are given a "weighting" in determining the amount of money from the state. As an example, a child who is in a full-time special education class may be "weighted" as 1.5, which means that for purposes of funding it is as-sumed that this student costs as much as 1.5 students in a regular edu-cation class. Or a student who leaves his or her regular classroom for help from a special education teacher or a speech therapist for only one class period a day may be weighted as 1.1 or 1.2, a recognition that the school district is obliged to pay more for the education of that student.

Another way of documenting the funding of special education stu-dents is to track costs. When the costs for educating a special education student exceed a certain level of cost determined by the state (this might be an amount that is double or triple the cost of educating a reg-ular education student), additional funding may be granted to the school district. All of the costs associated with these students must be documented carefully: salaries, tuition, special supplies and equipment, and so forth. At least the states are trying to address this problem. Since special education aid can provide a large amount of money to the school district it is imperative that the change leader keep accurate track of these things.

Level of disability. If the change leader has a program including stu-dents with disabilities it will probably be important for that change leader to know the percentage of time that each special education stu-dent is in a special education setting. For instance, if a student is only in a special education class, never in a regular education class, that stu-dent will be in special education 100 percent of the time. If a student spends an hour or a half hour per day with a resource teacher, but re-turns to a regular education class for the rest of the time, the percent-age of time is proportionally less. Some formulas will depend on the percentage of time a child is in a special education setting. Check with your business administrator. The level of disability may also relate to the weighting of a student.

FRPL. This acronym (pronounced *fur-pul*) stands for Free and Re-duced Price Lunch. The FRPL number is expressed as a percentage, as

in: "The district has a FRPL of 24.3 percent." This means that 24.3 percent of the students enrolled in the schools of the district are eligible to
receive free or reduced price meals. The FRPL number is used in a
number of determinations, both federal and state, to demonstrate the
level of student need in the district.

The federal government sponsors a school lunch and school breakfast program if a district chooses to participate in it. Students whose
households meet certain income guidelines may receive free meals
from the schools, or meals at a greatly reduced price. If a district par-
ticipates, then the district must go through a yearly qualifying procedure to see which students are eligible to receive lunch without cost and
which ones are eligible to pay a reduced price. Parents and/or guardians
must apply for this benefit, which requires that parents and/or
guardians must share income information with the school district. Immediately one can see some of the problems that are bound to occur.
Parents may be uncomfortable sharing confidential income information
with school officials. In addition, even though it is illegal for the school
district to identify recipients of free or reduced price lunches and break-
fasts in any way, students are very observant. They will note a student
who never has to pay cash for lunch or breakfast. It can become a
source of embarrassment for some students in some districts to even
use the free and reduced price lunch program, particularly at the secondary and middle school levels.

A problem for the district that derives from this is that funding for
many state and federal programs uses this FRPL percentage as an indicator of poverty. The higher the FRPL percentage, the greater the
poverty in the district and the more money that the district should receive because of the greater need that the FRPL count indicates. The
district business administrator will want to have this FRPL number as
accurate as possible and as high as possible in order to receive more
funds. Therefore the change leader will need to be alert to the possibility of students who may not be receiving benefits, but who are,
nonetheless, eligible. One of the quirks of the FRPL percentage, however, is that this number is based on a count of students, not on usage.
To become part of the FRPL percentage a student has to apply and be
approved, but never has to use the benefit. If a school has one hundred
students and twenty-five apply and are approved for FRPL, the per-

centage used in formulas is 25 percent. If all twenty-five of those students use the FRPL benefit or if only ten of those students use the benefit, the effect on funding remains the same.

The problem of applying for and using FRPL benefits is exacerbated at the secondary level. Students at this level, because of peer pressure, do not want to be classified as "in need" or in any way different from their peers. It is a function of the adolescent age, where no one wants to stand out from his or her peers in any way. The challenge is to ensure that these eligible students at least apply for the benefits. As many students as possible who are eligible must be encouraged to apply.

English Language Learners. This is the latest educational term that refers to students whose first language is not English. Another term that the change leader will hear is English as a Second Language students. They may be recent immigrants or have grown up in a community that is linguistically isolated from the public school system. These students will require special teachers to teach English as a second language or special classes of immersion or sheltered English classes (classes where content is taught in English, but at a lower linguistic level, and there is support for the students in their native language). This is also an indicator of school district need. The more students who require this service, the more funds may be received. Some states will have categorical aid just for students of this type. As with the FRPL percentage, the change leader needs to identify any students who are eligible to receive these special services.

Expenditures. State aid will sometimes depend on the amount of money spent on a program during a previous year. This is one reason why the district's school business administrator will try to drive home to other administrators the importance of reporting expenses accurately. In the case of categorical aid, it is imperative to monitor and track expenses precisely. Tracking expenditures accurately is a part of the accountability to build trust as well as a way to maximize receipt of funds.

Hours of Service. Some formulas will require the leader of the program to account for the number of hours spent in a particular phase of the program. It may be a requirement that certain groups of students receive an hour a day of instruction in a specific area, like reading or math. The change leader and the other staff members working with the students will need to develop a way to keep track that, hopefully, is not too onerous a task. Because of state and federal requirements for academic intervention services, this can become a very important figure to monitor.

District Wealth. There are other aspects of state aid funding formulas that the change leader will probably never have to worry about but should understand. Sometimes district wealth is included in a formula. This could be income wealth or property wealth. *Income wealth* is the amount of money earned in a given year by all of the people living within the school district boundaries. *Property wealth* is the value of all of the property within the district, commercial and residential.

District Need. Some states will assign an index for district need based on the number of students who need special services of some type: academic intervention, English as a Second Language, and so on. If the change leader accurately keeps those numbers that were previously mentioned, this number will be accurate also.

Student Scores. While this may not seem to be within the purview of a book on finance, the achievement of students may well have an impact on funding or on the use of funds, as with No Child Left Behind (NCLB), where, theoretically, a district may lose a student and that student's proportional share of funds to another district or have to provide additional outside services. An event such as this could direct funds away from the effort to reform. This is simply a reminder that the student scores are important to track not only for achievement data but also to ensure that the maximum amount of money is available to be directed toward reform.

The change leader should know that these data points can be a part of the formulas, but each state will have its own requirements and formulas for transmitting state aid to the school districts. Therefore the change leader must go to the district school business administrator to become familiar with the parts of the formulas on which the change leader may have an effect. And from the point of view of the business administrator, it is much easier to begin a program with the correct criteria for data collection, such as student count, than to go back to the beginning of the program and re-create the necessary data when it is time to file a report with the state.

THE VOCABULARY OF ACCOUNTING AND STATE AID

Earlier in this book it was stated that the educator, and the change leader, has a responsibility to educate himself or herself on all aspects of reform, including educational finance. Educators can no longer claim that finance is not important in schools. This being the case, there are a few basic accounting concepts that will need to be defined. The following terms and concepts are the ones that the change leader will hear in conversations with the school district business administrator and will use in the administration of budgets.

School district money can be a *revenue* or an *expense* (or *expenditure*). Revenue is money coming into the district, and an expenditure is money that is being paid out.

Each state will have its own *chart of accounts* that the change leader will have to use when administering the budget for a district, a grant, a building, or even a program. All educational finance in the state is put into the format of the chart of accounts. A chart of accounts is a listing of numeric codes where each signifies something different to the school district business administrator and to the state's reporting agency. These numeric codes form budget codes. A *budget code* is an identifier for one particular type of expense or revenue. These budget codes are required to accurately document what type of expense that money is spent on. A budget code is made up of several *segments* (pieces). Each segment has a meaning in the state chart of accounts. Following are some of the terms that the change leader will hear and will need to use:

A *fund* is a separate account of money. (Note that the term "funds" is also used as a synonym for money.) School districts operate on fund accounting, which means that at the year end, the balance in a fund (the bottom line) should be zero. Most of the money from state aid is kept in what is called the general fund or operations fund. This is the place for day-to-day moneys that support the daily operation of the school district. Money for categorical aid may be maintained in a separate fund where it can be tracked and accounted for separately from the district's general operating moneys. Cafeteria operations are also kept separately as are funds for a school store or other business run by the students.

A *fund balance* is the amount of money remaining in a fund at the end of the school year or grant period. In its simplest form the fund balance is the amount of revenue minus the amount of expenditures. However, a fund balance can be positive or negative. A positive fund balance means that the fund has a *surplus* of money, where a negative fund balance indicates a *deficit* of funds. As the administrator of a grant or program, the change leader does not want to find that program with a negative fund balance. That is why it is so important to accurately and frequently monitor expenditures.

A *function* or *program* is a numeric designation that tells what job within the district the money is being spent to support. The state will have a list of functions that it uses. Examples of some of the functions of a school district would be: regular education, special education, transportation, operations of building, or board of education.

Object is the part of the budget code that the change leader will probably be most concerned with. The object code indicates what kind of thing the money will be spent for within the larger functional area of the budget. Those basic areas of expense are: salaries, benefits, equipment, purchased services, and supplies.

Some school districts will use a *location* or *instructional unit* code to indicate in which building an expense is made. This is also sometimes referred to as an expense center or cost center.

Large districts may wish to use a *departmental* or *program* code, which classifies expenses even further. For instance, the change leader may wish to segregate expenses for summer programs or department expenses at the secondary level.

With a little practice the change leader will be able to read a full budget code in the same way that he or she can read a sentence in a book. This is an example from the New York State Chart of Accounts: A 2110 200 01.

Looking at each part of the budget code, the change leader can tell that: this expense is from unrestricted money, so there are no special rules for spending it (A, general fund); the expense is for instruction (2110, regular education); the expense is for equipment (200, equipment); and it is being spent at XYZ school (01, location code). Each state's chart of accounts can be deciphered and used in this same manner.

In all cases the change leader should seek the help of the district's business administrator to learn about coding and the aspects of accounting that will apply to a given program. Each state has specific names for each part of a budget code, but basically the budget code will indicate the area in the district where the expense is taking place (instruction, operations and maintenance, etc.) and what kind of expense it is (salaries, equipment, supplies, etc.). It will be particularly important to know and to share the information of budget coding in administering one's own budget.

HOW TO USE THE MONEY TO FINANCE A REFORM PROGRAM

By now the reader may be wondering why this chapter has given so much detail on financial topics that are applicable to *traditional* educational programs and to the concept of state aid as a whole. The answer is that if you know the information and how it applies to traditional educational programs, you will be able to manipulate it and direct it for use in educational reform programs also, and the district will have the maximum amount of money available to apply to that reform. But it is more than just knowing how to manipulate numbers that is important. Use of state money to finance reform goes back to chapter 1 and the five basic qualities for effective use of funding that were mentioned there.

All of the qualities mentioned are important. As a user of state aid money, the change leader must exhibit all of the attributes of trustworthiness. Integrity is necessary in using the money properly, according to sound accounting practices, and in issues of compliance if you are dealing with categorical aid. The change leader must be accountable for the decisions that he or she has made in a program by reporting regularly on finances and educational outcomes, and he or she must honor the idea of decentralized decision making. Naturally, the lines of communication must be open within the district and to outside groups. But above all, the change leader has to have *focus*. Without focus the money can be frittered away on things that do not support the reform that the change leader is trying to implement.

For instance, if the money from the state is in the form of categorical aid, the money must be used to finance the program for which it is intended, but the change leader can, however, within the categorical program, change the direction or thrust of what is happening in the program.

As an example, take a categorical program for English as a Second Language (ESL). The state requires that the money be spent for students who are learning English. What the change leader must do is focus the effort. Some districts might interpret such an ESL program as an after-school program for homework help or English classes, but what if the reform that has been identified as the focus for the district is mathematics achievement? Focusing the use of the categorical money requires the same process outlined in chapter 1 of looking at the needs of the students. In this example the change leader would look at the students projected to be in this ESL program. How do the scores of these students compare to those of the school or grade level as a whole? Does this group score lower on math tests than the rest of the grade level? If so, then tailor the program to work on those math skills. Would it be more helpful to have the additional services during the school day? Is there time available? What would be the impact of doing that on the rest of the students and the remainder of the student day?

Once the change leader has identified the needs and the time frame, he or she must spend the money in a way that addresses those needs. If a program is designed to help math skills, going to a baseball game as a field trip to have fun or to motivate or bribe students may not be a good use of money or time. If everyone is doing statistics on the players, doing geometry with the layout of the baseball diamond, and so forth, then that is a good use of the field trip. Take every advantage of the opportunities to address the academic need that the program has been developed to address. Just remember that it does not need to be boring, dry, or no fun, but the change leader and staff members may need to be creative.

The change leader must be sure that he or she is familiar with what the categorical money may be spent on. If that field trip to a baseball game is not permitted under the rules of the aid, no matter what great mathematical concepts are taught, you cannot do it. Or at least you cannot pay for the trip with categorical funds. If the change leader is not familiar with these parameters, it is necessary to go to the school business administrator to get the rules for spending this categorical money.

If the change leader is using general state aid money, the job becomes much easier. It is necessary to simply follow the procedures to focus the use of the money. The parameters on expenditures in this case will be the parameters set up by the district in terms of how to spend the money and how to account for it. Here the business administrator may give the change leader guidelines for purchasing, bidding, time sheets, and so on.

In keeping with the admonition for focus on reform, the change leader *must not*, and this cannot be said too often or too strongly, run a program just because it has "always been done this way"! Evaluate the needs of the particular group of students who will be in the program. Don't waste the student time, the change leader's time, and the money that could be used on an effective reform program!

HOW SHOULD THE IDEAL STATE AID FORMULA BE STRUCTURED?

It is safe for the change leader to assume that current state aid formulas are not ideal. As indicated previously, these funding formulas many times are the result of political compromise rather than what is best for schools, students, or reform. In many states, funding formulas are incredibly complex, and in many cases are based on criteria other than the need of the district to receive funds to support the basic education guaranteed to all students or the needs of the students in trying to reach standards of achievement.

An example of a state aid formula that is currently in use in New York State reads like this:

Comprehensive Operating Aid: This is the sum of 2002–03 Comprehensive Operating Aid, Gifted and Talented Aid, Operating Standards Aid and Academic Support Aid and the 2003–04 Operating Aid Reduction. The 2003–04 Operating Aid Reduction is a reduction factor applied to the above listed four aids. The factor is the sum of 0.0175 and a need/resource-adjusted 0.0810, with the result expressed as a negative decimal. The need/resource adjustment is the product of the positive result of 0.95 minus the 2001–02 free and reduced-price lunch ratio multiplied by the CWR. The factor has a minimum of -0.0225 and a maximum of $-.0630$ (i.e., the reduction is between 2.25 and 6.3 percent). (New York State Department of Education)

This is the formula for basic operating aid, the money that can be used most widely and therefore a very important aid. At least the FRPL number, which indicates need, is included as part of the formula. Clearly some refinement is needed if the state is to have understandable criteria for distributing state money.

For years now groups of citizens have been filing suit against states claiming that the formulas used to distribute money are unfair, or are inadequate to provide for the free public education that is promised to all children. Ohio, Michigan, Florida, New York, Kentucky, New Jersey, Vermont, and Maryland are just a few of the states that have tried to rework funding formulas.

In all cases legislatures have had to back up and go through the process once again of negotiating state aid formulas, hopefully in a more equitable way, but with mixed success in reality. The operative phrase, however, is that of "negotiating school aid formulas." It would be more equitable if the aid were based on some sort of objective criteria so that it could not be modified at will or negotiated. It is widely agreed that a truly equitable state aid formula would have two very important criteria: it would be based on need, both need of students and need of the district, and it would make available to each district an adequate amount of money to provide a free, basic education. One example of this "ideal" is a formula from the Midstate School Finance Consortium in New York State, and the concepts in that formula are presented here. While this is not the be-all and end-all of aid formulas, it demonstrates how a formula that is simple and based on the two basic criteria of need and adequacy can help reform by directing state funds to districts and to areas of greatest need.

The ideal formula starts by providing enough money per student to cover the cost of a basic education. Determining the cost of a basic education can be problematic, since costs and definitions of a basic education vary widely across a given state. But regional costs can be adjusted so that the expense for a basic education can be determined statewide. What a basic education comprises may be a bit more difficult because of different perceptions. A board of education in one district may see a basic education as the three Rs, "reading, 'riting, and 'rithmetic," while the district next door or close by may consider art, instrumental music, or choreography as a part of that basic education.

Each state has to determine this for itself, but in general, the things that the state education department mandates define the basic education in a state. It makes sense to assume that if a state wants a certain subject taught to a certain level, the state should be willing to fund the expenses for teaching that subject across the state.

For the purposes of demonstrating the effect of a need-based funding formula rather than a politically negotiated one, eight thousand dollars will be assumed as the yearly cost of educating a child to the level mandated by the state.

Once the statewide cost for a basic education is determined, that cost can be adjusted by regional factors. For instance, in school districts near New York City, the cost of living and the costs of construction and salaries are higher than the costs associated with a rural community far from a major city. Therefore the cost of providing a basic education is modified by this regional factor to account for differences in cost of living.

In table 2.1 an example of the effect of this regional factor is shown. Starting with the assumption that the average cost of educating a student is eight thousand dollars, a school district located in an area with a higher than average cost of living would be recognized as having a higher cost of education. A school district in an area with a lower cost of living index would have a lower cost for basic education.

Once the modified cost per student is determined, the number of all students attending public schools in the district must be used as a multiplier. (This number is enrollment, not attendance.) Since each child is guaranteed a basic education, a district must have this much money available to provide that basic education for all students. In table 2.2 one can see how the total amount of funds needed is calculated, assuming that the three districts compared have the same number of students.

Table 2.1.   The Effect of Regional Cost Factor Adjustment

	Average Regional Cost of Living	More Expensive Regional Cost of Living	Less Expensive Regional Cost of Living
Cost of a Basic Education per Student	$8,000	$8,000	$8,000
Regional Cost Factor	1.0	1.1	0.9
Cost of a Basic Education Modified by the Regional Cost Factor	$8,000	$8,800.00	$7,200.00

Table 2.2.   Calculation of Total Operating Aid

	Average Regional Cost of Living	More Expensive Regional Cost of Living	Less Expensive Regional Cost of Living
Cost of a Basic Education Modified by the Regional Cost Factor	$8,000	$8,800	$7,200
Number of Students Enrolled in District	1,000	1,000	1,000
Total Operating Cost	$8,000,000	$8,800,000	$7,200,000

The district that is in an area where the cost of living is higher will receive a larger amount of money per student; the district in an area where the cost of living is less will receive less.

But it is also fair to expect that a local district should contribute to the education of its students. A level of local funding must be determined. In this formula it is a set minimum tax rate. The change leader will be familiar with the expression of this example: "Thirteen dollars per thousand." This means simply that for each thousand dollars in property value, the owner of that property must pay thirteen dollars. In a different formula a different measure could be used. The minimum tax rate is applied to the property value in the district to determine the amount of local contribution, and that local effort is deducted from the cost of a basic education so that the state and the local district are sharing the costs of that basic education. In table 2.3 the effect of that local contribution on three districts is shown. The local effort is a constant across the property value of the district. In table 2.3 it is assumed that each district has the same operating expense per student so that the reader can see how property wealth affects the amount of money received. Local effort for this example is assumed to be thirteen dollars

Table 2.3.   The Effect of Local Effort

	Average Property Wealth	Greater Property Wealth	Lesser Property Wealth
Total Operating Cost	$8,000,000	$8,000,000	$8,000,000
Property Value	$50,000,000	$70,000,000	$30,000,000
Local Effort Rate	$13 per thousand	$13 per thousand	$13 per thousand
Local Effort Amount	$650,000	$910,000	$390,000
Total Operating Aid to Be Contributed by the State	$7,350,000	$7,090,000	$7,610,000

per thousand dollars of property value. It can be seen that the greater the property wealth of a district, the greater is its ability to raise taxes to support the schools, so the state aid contribution is reduced.

The change leader should note that the numerical amount for the value of property only seems large when one is talking about that value. After all, fifty million dollars—the amount of property value in the district of average property wealth—appears to be a lot of property value. However, if one thinks about the cost of a house or property, it is easy to see how the total amount of assessed property value arrives at such a high figure. If all of the properties in a school district were valued at one hundred thousand dollars each, a fifty million dollar total for property value would be only five hundred properties at that one hundred thousand dollar value. The values used in the examples in this chapter are for the sake of illustration only.

After the allowance for local effort, the formula should address the needs of students who require additional services because of disabilities, placement in special education classes, language problems, and so on. To do this, each district has to have an accurate count of how many enrolled students have special needs. Some of the criteria for special needs in a given needs-based formula may be: need for ESL services, need for academic intervention services, FRPL, or special education services. In the Midstate School Finance Consortium formula the count for students with extraordinary needs is modified by how wealthy a district is, as compared to the state average. A district that is of average wealth will receive a predetermined amount of money for each child deemed to be "at risk." A district that is wealthier than most will receive less money for each at-risk student, and a district that is poorer than the average will receive more money for each at-risk student. In this way the needs of the students and the needs of the district are both addressed.

Average wealth is defined as a district that has an amount of wealth, property and/or income, that is close to the average for the state. A district of greater wealth will have more property and income; a district of lesser wealth will have less. The wealth factor can be expressed as a number, where the district of average need has a wealth factor of 1.0, a wealthier district will have a wealth factor exceeding 1.0, and a poorer district will have a wealth factor less than 1.0. In this formula the

amount of money allocated for students with extraordinary needs is calculated by dividing the number of students with those needs by the
wealth factor. This modified student count is then multiplied by a predetermined amount of money per student.

The amount of money that is allocated per student because of these
extraordinary needs is determined statewide by a standard of reason-
ableness. Experts in school finance all agree that it is more expensive
to educate some students than to educate others, so a reasonable percentage increase is decided for this type of student. In any given formula it can be 10, 15, or 20 percent. In this example it is 10 percent additional money. It can be seen in table 2.4 how a district of lesser wealth
will receive more money for extraordinary needs, and a district with
greater wealth will receive less.

The amount to cover the basic education, minus the local effort, and
the amount needed to cover the cost for at-risk students are added together. This becomes the district's state aid number. It will fluctuate
from year to year based on enrollment and on need.

There are certain expenses that are not expected to be covered in this
formula. Students who have severe handicapping conditions and are in
special schools, the cost of constructing new school buildings, and
other aids unique to the state are calculated separately and transmitted
to each district.

This is a simple formula based on need and wealth (or lack of it).
What could be easier and more logical? An example of how the total
formula would work in different districts is given in table 2.5.

Please note that all districts are assumed to have the same number of
students enrolled in the district and the same number of students who

Table 2.4.   Students with Extraordinary Needs and the Wealth Factor

	Average Wealth	Greater Wealth	Lesser Wealth
Number of Students with			
Extraordinary Needs	200	200	200
District Wealth Factor	1.0	1.3	0.6
Number of Students Divided			
by the District Wealth Factor	200.00	153.85	333.33
Extraordinary Needs Basic			
Allotment Per Student	$800.00	$800.00	$800.00
Total State Aid for			
Extraordinary Needs	$160,000.00	$123,076.92	$266,666.67

Table 2.5.   Total Calculation of State Aid

		District A	District B	District C
1.	Cost of a Basic Education per Student	$8,000.00	$8,000.00	$8,000.00
2.	Regional Cost Factor	1.0	1.1	0.9
3.	Cost of a Basic Education per Student Modified by the Regional Cost Factor	$8,000.00	$8,800.00	$7,200.00
4.	Number of Students Enrolled in District	1,000	1,000	1,000
5.	Total Operating Cost	$8,000,000.00	$8,800,000.00	$7,200,000.00
6.	Property Value in District	$50,000,000.00	$70,000,000.00	$30,000,000.00
7.	Local Effort Rate	$13 per thousand	$13 per thousand	$13 per thousand
8.	Local Effort Amount	$650,000.00	$910,000.00	$390,000.00
9.	Operating Aid to Be Contributed by the State	$7,350,000.00	$7,890,000.00	$6,810,000.00
10.	Number of Students with Extraordinary Needs	200	200	200
11.	District Wealth Factor	1.0	1.1	0.9
12.	Number of Extraordinary Need Students Divided by the District Wealth Factor	200.00	181.82	222.22
13.	Extraordinary Needs Basic Allotment	$800.00	$800.00	$800.00
14.	Total Aid for Extraordinary Needs	$160,000.00	$145,454.55	$177,777.78
15.	Grand Total State Aid	$7,510,000.00	$8,035,454.55	$6,987.777.78

have extraordinary needs. District A is an average district and can be used for comparison purposes. In District A the cost of providing an education is at the average cost statewide. District A also has an average amount of wealth and property, as compared to the rest of the state. Therefore the adjusting factors, or regional cost and district wealth, both are 1.0 and will not modify the formula.

District B could be found in a suburb near a large city. It has a cost of education that is higher than the state average (regional cost factor of 1.1); therefore the amount of money that is necessary to provide education is increased (line 3). However, because of greater district wealth (district wealth factor of 1.1), the amount of money that the state contributes for students with extraordinary needs is lowered (line 14).

District C could be found in a rural area. The cost of providing an education in this district is lower than the state average (regional cost factor of 0.9); therefore the amount of money that is necessary to provide education is lower also (line 3). Decreased district wealth (district wealth factor of 0.9) increases the amount of money that the state contributes for students with extraordinary needs (line 14).

Of course, there are multiple permutations of factors that can be included in an example of this formula, but one can see that with a formula of this type, a district with the highest cost of student education receives more state aid and a district with the highest student need receives more aid. The change leader can see that a formula that relies on student need, the cost of an adequate education, and district need will drive the money to the areas of greatest need. If states were to adopt a formula that was need based, the change leader would be able to spend more of his or her time on instructional issues rather than financial. Unfortunately many states have not arrived at this conclusion yet.

THINGS TO ASK THE DISTRICT'S SCHOOL BUSINESS ADMINISTRATOR

As indicated, the change leader should develop a working relationship with the school district business administrator. The business office can be a valuable resource in educating the change leader as to the data that needs to be captured as well as the restrictions on spending money. These are some of the questions that the change leader should ask:

Is this program part of a categorical aid package? If so, what is the amount of categorical aid received? How much of that aid is to be used for this project?

What expenses are under the supervision of the change leader?

What student information needs to be monitored and maintained in order to report this program accurately and with the least amount of frustration? Is it attendance reporting? Is it service hours?

What financial information needs to be monitored? What are the district rules for purchasing items? Are there special rules for spending this money either from the district or from the state?

What compliance issues need to be monitored for accurate reporting from the business office? (There may be a separate reporting that has to be maintained in an instruction or curriculum office.)

For a change leader, the school business administrator can be a valuable resource and a font of financial information.

SUMMARY

State aid funding is an area where the change leader has less control than in others, but also where the change leader can exercise his or her skills for maximizing existing income. Accurate data reporting can maximize the amount of money received by a school district, making more total money available and, therefore, more money that can be directed to reform efforts.

The problem here is that the states and their legislatures are deciding what is an important program and what is not. Although their collective heart may be in the right place, can politicians who are noneducators decide which programs are important by manipulating the funding received? Should they?

Since current funding formulas are based, in many cases, on political negotiations, the ultimate goal of the change leader should be to help his or her state achieve a state funding formula that is based on need, both of students and of the district, and on the actual cost of providing a basic education. An example of this type of formula is from the Midstate School Finance Consortium in New York State. A need-based formula will respond to needs in allotting state aid rather than responding to political issues; it is more of a student-based formula.

As with all areas of educational finance, the change leader should develop a relationship with the school district business office and the administrator who supervises it. Working with the district business office from the beginning of a school year, or even prior to a new school year, can lead to a much smoother reporting year for both the business office and the change leader.

CHAPTER 3

Using Federal Funding to Support Educational Reform

For many years the federal government has been providing money to support educational programs in the schools, most notably ESEA (the Elementary and Secondary Education Act). This act provides funding for specific programs in schools; these funds are often referred to as entitlement grants. With an entitlement grant each school district has access to this money by virtue of legislation, not by virtue of a competitive process. The federal government decides the overall amount of money that is allotted to these grants, then divides that money among the states. The states are then responsible for transmitting the money to the school districts within that state. The formula that determines how much money each district receives is based on the number of students in the individual district who meet certain criteria for poverty, risk factors, or disability. The district is therefore "entitled" to the money, thus the term *entitlement grants*. The positive side of this for the change leader is that there is a much simpler process for applying for these federal funds than for a competitive grant. The negative is that the district cannot increase the amount of money received to exceed the allotment from the government.

The change leader should note here, however, that there are competitive components to some of the federal "entitlement grants," such as Twenty-First Century Learning Community Grants. The school district grants coordinator or the state education department will be able to assist the change leader who is seeking to qualify for one of these competitive grants. The competitive aspects of federal grants must be treated in the same way as other competitive grants, as shown in chapter 5. This chapter will refer only to the entitlement portion of the federal grants.

NO CHILD LEFT BEHIND

The 2001 reauthorization of ESEA (the Elementary and Secondary Education Act) is more commonly referred to as the No Child Left Behind Act, or NCLB in the day-to-day parlance of educators. With the passage of NCLB it appears that the federal government is becoming very serious about the need to improve education in this country. Perhaps the legislators were spurred by the same impetus that drives educational reformers, that is, the failure of public schools to remake themselves to provide better educational services. Whatever the motivation may have been, changes have been mandated by law in how education is delivered when federal funds pay for it. Whether this is an appropriate role for the federal government to play or not is a conversation to be held in another venue. Right now, however, No Child Left Behind is the reality within which schools must operate. At the very least the change leader needs to learn about these changes and ensure that the district receives its allocated funds. Even more important is to ensure that those funds are spent most effectively to improve education.

The changes in regulation that are proving to be most problematic for some districts are the changes regarding the maintenance of highly qualified staff. In many areas there has been and continues to be a shortage of certified teachers, particularly in subjects like the sciences, mathematics, and foreign language. No Child Left Behind has set a deadline for all districts to meet by which time all teachers are required to be highly qualified. Highly qualified is defined as possessing three things: (1) certification appropriate for the subject area in which the staff member teaches, (2) a passing grade on the appropriate test for teaching in the certification area, and (3), for secondary teachers, demonstrated competence in the area in which they are certified. Each state has its own detailed definition of highly qualified staff and its own plan for helping districts and teachers achieve this level of qualification. After the NCLB-imposed deadline, districts will no longer be able to use teachers who have temporary licenses, nor will teachers be able to teach outside of their certification area.

Paraprofessionals also have come under regulation of NCLB. Paraprofessionals will be required to have at least a two-year degree and demonstrate competence in assisting in the area to which they are assigned. For these staff members each state will also have a plan for reaching the goal of highly qualified staff.

As with all new laws and regulations, the procedures for implementation are being worked out on a daily basis. There are some provisions for special circumstances, but to receive accurate information the change leader must check with the state education department in his or her state. The change leader will find that the states will vary in their interpretation of these regulations.

To emphasize the seriousness of the governmental commitment to No Child Left Behind legislation, the federal government is now threatening sanctions for individual schools and districts that do not comply with the NCLB mandates and standards. That noncompliance could be in the area of qualification of staff, as mentioned above, or it could be regarding test scores and the failure to reach Adequate Yearly Progress (AYP) in a district. Each state has determined a standard for Adequate Yearly Progress in the school districts of that state. A goal and a deadline have been set. Districts must demonstrate progress toward that goal each year or face sanctions. In addition, falling behind in AYP means that there is a larger amount of progress that must be shown the following year.

As an example of what this means for a school district, the plan toward achieving AYP in a hypothetical district might look something like this: Assume that a state has set a goal that 80 percent of all students in the fourth grade reach the proficiency level on a given test in ten years. A district that currently has 40 percent of its students in that proficient category would have to increase the percentage of students who scored at the proficient level by 4 percent each year. If, in one year, the scores in that category only increase by 2 percent, in the following year the example district will have to increase scores in the proficient category by 6 percent to maintain adequate yearly progress, perhaps making it even more difficult for the district to reach that AYP standard.

Districts can also be deemed to be subject to sanctions if the district or a school is considered persistently dangerous, meaning that there is a large number of disciplinary incidents, particularly ones involving the use of weapons. You will see later in this chapter that there is now a requirement for reporting these incidents and many of the statistics that are related to this issue.

Sanctions include simple notification and inclusion on a warning list, or the government can become involved in mandating very specific use of funds. More serious sanctions will require districts to pay for supplemental educational services for students or even send students and accompanying funds to neighboring districts. The change leader must check with the state education department for specific guidelines.

While it is always a welcome experience for a school district to receive money from the government, money from the government does not come without some strings attached. There is a very real danger that if a school district doesn't follow the regulations that have been established for these grants, that district will lose federal money. Of course, if a district objected strongly enough to the additional regulations of the No Child Left Behind Act, that district would have the option of no longer accepting federal funds. Not many school districts have this option, however.

APPLYING FOR ENTITLEMENT FUNDS

To receive moneys under No Child Left Behind, a school district must complete and submit an extensive application document called the Consolidated Application, which will serve as the application for all of the ESEA entitlement grants. The district will only receive money for the individual grants, however, if it is eligible for those moneys. This same application must be submitted whether a district is eligible for all ESEA grants, or for only one.

The grants school districts most commonly receive from ESEA are:

- Title I. This is a fund to support disadvantaged children, and is generally the largest of the ESEA grants that a district receives. Remedial programs and support services can be funded from this grant.
- Title II-A, Preparing, Training, and Recruiting High-Quality Teachers and Principals. This aspect provides money for recruitment, training, professional development, merit pay, and other methods of attracting and retaining highly qualified staff members in a school.

- Title II-D, Enhancing Education through Technology. This provides funds for the support of technology programs in the school district, including professional development.
- Title III, Language Instruction for Limited English Proficient. This entitlement is given to districts that have students who are deficient in the skills of speaking English. It is a per-child subsidy based on the number of students in the school's demographic who meet this criterion.
- Title IV, Safe and Drug-Free Schools. This money is used for programs that enhance the safety and health of the students. Programs that may be funded include violence prevention, counseling, and even surveillance.
- Title V, Innovative Programs. This allows funds to be used for proven programs that have been shown to increase the achievement of the students.

In applying for grants under the No Child Left Behind Act, the change leader should be aware of a number of statistics that, while not purely financial, may affect the amount of money received in the entitlement grants. While the change leader may not personally track all of these areas of statistics, he or she must know where to locate this information in order to apply for these grants. The change leader will find that a good system of student accountability and tracking will be very valuable in this area. The ability to maintain and to disaggregate student data is essential.

Although this is not an exhaustive list, the student information that the change leader will be required to present may include the following demographic data:

- Enrollment by grade
- Enrollment by race and gender
- The percentage of students on free lunch and the percentage of students on reduced lunch (the numbers may have to be reported separately)
- The number of students with a deficiency in English
- The percentage of students in single-parent homes
- The number and percentage of students repeating a grade

- The tardy rate of the school/district and the absenteeism rate of the school/district
- The percentage of students who are suspended, promoted, or who receive detention
- The drop-out rate
- The number of disciplinary incidents in a year (naturally the problem here is in the definition of a disciplinary incident: definitions vary, and clear guidelines have not been forthcoming from the federal government), along with the number of victims, the number of offenders, and how many incidents occurred on school property

NCLB is also looking for data on parental statistics—how many parents attend student conferences, and how many parents volunteer—as well as types of community support and business partnerships.

For students who have special education needs, the application requires the number of students receiving various services (occupational therapy, physical therapy, speech, counseling, etc.), the number of students eligible for Medicaid, the number of students referred to the building-level assistance team, and the number of students who have been referred to that team but are awaiting assessment.

Even the number of prekindergarten students and Head Start students may need to be counted and identified, along with kindergarteners who have had the Head Start experience.

Along with the narrative and demographic data that is requested, the district must submit a budget for each grant for which it is eligible. Once the Consolidated Application is approved, the budget that was submitted with the Consolidated Application becomes the formal budget for the grant(s) for which the district applied. It is therefore very important that the estimated budget submitted with the Consolidated Application be created as realistically and as accurately as possible, just like a budget for the full general fund. Budgets for the grants will be discussed later in this chapter in the section on finances.

FOCUS AND THE ENTITLEMENT GRANTS

The federal government has been very specific in telling the districts not only how to apply for entitlement moneys, but also how to use

them. It is the job of the change leader to ensure that within the parameters of the individual entitlement grant, the money is used to support the reform of the district.

As has been discussed previously in this book, a program that is already in effect in a district tends to remain in effect ad infinitum. This
is the "we've always done it that way" syndrome. In many places this
has happened with the entitlement grants also. A program is established, is identified as Title I (or some other grant), and then takes on
a life of its own. As long as there are sufficient Title I funds to support the program, no one has had to evaluate the program in terms of
effectiveness. With the impetus of No Child Left Behind and high-
stakes testing, the change leader now has to review these Title programs to determine, first, if they are effective and, second, if these
programs fit into the plan of reform for the school district. If there is
a Title I reading program, for instance, that does not produce either an
increase in test scores or better readers, the change leader must evaluate the program to ascertain the reason why the program is not succeeding. It may even be decided that the program should be termi-
nated, regardless of how long it has been in place. Then the change
leader is able to find a program that will be effective and support that
program with the funds that had previously been used to support the
ineffective program.

One issue that the change leader will need to be aware of is that of
"supplement versus supplant." The federal government from time to
time will perform an audit of a district's federal grants. In this way it
can monitor compliance with all regulations, operational and financial.
One of the things that the government will look at is the issue of supplanting district programs. Federal moneys are designated for particular programs to support particular federal goals. To use that federal
money to support programs that a district would normally provide anyway is "supplanting" district programs. The federal money instead
should be used to "supplement" district programs.

As an example of an instance of "supplement versus supplant," look
at a mathematics program in a school district: Every district is obliged
to offer a program of instruction in mathematics, and district funds pay
for that program. When that district receives Title I funds, those federal funds should not be used to pay for the basic math program that is

already in place. Instead, those funds should be used to supplement the existing math program, by doing things like buying remedial math materials, hiring special teachers to give extra assistance to students who need that help, or purchasing computer programs that allow for mathematics practice and ongoing assessment. These materials and actions supplement the district program. The government auditors will be seeking documentation that the federal funds are used to supplement the district programs, not supplant them.

Another way to supplement district programs rather than to supplant them, but also a way to move as much monetary support as possible to the district reform, is to focus all of the federal moneys on the reform. Have the different Title grants work together. In the same example as given above with the mathematics reform, the change leader could use Title I money to hire additional mathematics specialists and teacher assistants. Title II-A could pay for professional development for math teachers or elementary teachers who are teaching math. Title V (Innovative Programs) could buy math materials from proven programs that have been shown to be successful; Title II-D could help with technology purchases where computer programs could be used to supplement the math program. Using all Title funds in concert with each other to reach the district's reform goals is an effective use of the money as the change leader seeks to promote reform in his or her district.

Before attempting to coordinate all grants, though, the change leader should perform a complete needs assessment for the district, as recommended in chapter 1. If this has already been done for the district, a great deal of effort has been saved for the change leader. Remember that the needs assessment, and therefore the use of funds, must be based on the data, not feelings, and must be aligned with the state standards for students. If all of the students in a district score well on, say, the social studies assessment but not on science, it is not an effective use of money to supplement the social studies program. It would make more sense to supplement science.

Once it is possible to take a look at the district as a whole and to know what the weaknesses are in the education being delivered, and exactly where those weaknesses are, the change leader can use the federal grant money according to regulations, but to support the work of the general fund money.

This does not mean, however, that a school district can never change the use of the federal entitlement money, or change the allocation of that money to different expense categories. It is possible to change these items by simply filing an amendment prior to the changes taking place. Check with the state education department in the individual state for regulations and guidelines on doing so in that state.

THE ACCOUNTABILITY ASPECT OF THE ENTITLEMENT GRANTS

At the risk of seeming redundant, the question of financial accountability in using public money always goes back to the attributes in chapter 1. The change leader must build trust within the public that the money from federal grants is being spent wisely. The money to fund these grants, while it is from the federal government, is not a gift without cost. As in the case of state aid, the money actually comes from the pockets of the taxpayers. The taxpayers pay the federal government, and some of that money is returned to the school districts in the form of these entitlement grants. The school district is still spending public money when using these grants, so the public needs to feel confident that this money is not being wasted or spent ineffectively.

In some school districts, the school district constituencies have had no information as to how these federal moneys were spent, but the regulations in the No Child Left Behind legislation now require that parents, as well as other groups in the districts, sign off on the use of funds, and that sign-off is part of the grant application, so the use of the federal moneys must be well communicated to all of the constituencies in the learning community, using the bases of clear and honest communication. The regulations that apply to federal moneys and their use may seem confusing even to educators. The challenge for the change leader is to make these regulations comprehensible to the noneducators in order to garner public support for the programs and, in turn, for the reform of the school district.

Accountability for the proper use of the federal money requires integrity. Since uses of this money are strictly prescribed, the change leader must ensure that these funds are used only as they should be. If an expense or a program is not allowed under the rules and regulations of a grant, it is incumbent upon the change leader to see to it that this expense is not allowed. This requires that the change leader train all administrators and that the administrators, in turn, pass that information on to the teachers in the schools. And not just the teachers who are using the money, but all of the teachers, so that everyone understands.

At the end of the grant period, the school district will have to file with the federal government to show that it has, indeed, performed the actions and spent the money as it projected on the Consolidated Application. Failure to meet this standard of accountability can result in loss of the federal moneys for that fiscal year or even of future funds. The accountability piece of the entitlement grants is a very important aspect.

FINANCES AND THE ENTITLEMENT GRANTS

This is the section of the chapter that one would expect to see in a book on financing educational reform; this is the part of the chapter that will give the change leader the knowledge to enable him or her to budget grants, monitor grants, and help the business office of the school district file the accountability forms at the end of the grant year.

Legislation requires that school districts account for money from the ESEA entitlement grants in a way that clearly identifies both the revenue and the expenditures as being a part of a particular grant. In some states there is even a special fund, called the *Special Aid Fund*, which is the place where grants are accounted for in the business office. Ethically, of course, federal funds, private grants, or other funds that are *restricted* (there are rules for what the funds may be spent on) should never be mixed with district operating funds. In terms of ease of reporting, funds that are maintained separately will allow for a faster reporting process because the revenues and expenditures for a given grant will not need to be researched and *reclassified* (identified as grant related).

Regardless of how the budget coding structure of the state is set up, the district should be able to identify not only the source of the money but also the particular grant that the money is for. The district should be able to produce a report that is divided into the separate sources of funds and the amount of funds from each of these sources; this report should be available from the financial accounting software in use in

Table 3.1.   Sources of Revenue for a School District

Fund (Revenue Source)	Amount of Revenue
General Fund	$4,807,913
Special Aid Fund—Title I	$231,800
Special Aid Fund—Title II-A	$37,000
Special Aid Fund—Title II-D	$7,809
Special Aid Fund—Title III	$118
Special Aid Fund—Title V	$5,003
Cafeteria Fund	$191,000

Note: Amounts are for example only and do not reflect an existing budget.

the district. Please see table 3.1 for an example of a simple report of this type.

At a glance the change leader is able to see the source of the revenue to support district programs. Remember that, in the district business office, the revenue and the expenses for each of these separate programs must be recorded separately.

In applying for the entitlement funds with the Consolidated Application, the change leader will be required to submit an estimated budget that reflects how he or she plans to use the money in each grant for which the district is eligible. The areas of expense that are used in applying for the federal grants are the same as used in the school district's general fund budget:

Professional staff (certificated)
Nonprofessional staff (support staff)
Benefits
Equipment (nontechnology)
Equipment (technology)
Purchased services
Supplies and materials (including textbooks)
Travel
Indirect costs

Indirect costs is an area that is unique to federal grants. It is clear that there is some time expended in preparing the grants, monitoring the grants, and filing for the grants. Not only is there time involved, but there is also the cost of copy paper, postage, use of the telephone, and so on used in that preparation. The indirect cost is a small percentage that the school district is allowed to take from the grant to cover the administrative costs of the grant. Indirect cost is not a constant. Each district must apply for its own indirect cost rate and each state will have guidelines and regulations for doing so. Again, check with the state education department.

In preparing the Consolidated Application, the change leader will have to submit a budget that estimates how the funds are going to be used, along with a narrative telling what the change leader hopes to accomplish by this use of the money. As an example, table 3.2 uses the Title I funds listed in table 3.1 to show how a change leader might allocate the money and explain the reasons behind those choices so that the reader will be able to see how the narrative and the budget need to be compatible with each other. (Please note that, because Title I is a grant, the amount of expenditures budgeted cannot exceed the amount of revenue that is expected.)

The change leader may not wish to use all of the categories that are available. In focusing the use of the money, the district should spend funds only where they are going to be effective.

In monitoring entitlement grant funds, the change leader will have to use all of the budget skills that he or she uses with the general fund moneys. During the fiscal year the change leader must be able to monitor the expenses from the grant. This can be accomplished by use of a

Table 3.2.   An Explanation of Costs Associated with a Grant

Budget Description	Amount	Narrative Information
Professional Staff	$80,000	Two reading teachers each earning $40,000 per year
Support Staff	$64,000	Four teacher assistants each earning $16,000 per year
Equipment (Nontechnology)	$1,000	Computer tables and chairs
Equipment (Technology)	$10,000	Five computers at $2,000 each
Purchased Services	$0	
Supplies and Materials	$29,210	XYZ software for reading comprehension practice and ongoing assessment ($20,000) Supplemental reading textbooks ($9,210)
Travel	$0	
Benefits	$36,000	Benefits for two reading teachers and four teacher assistants
Indirect Costs	$11,590	5 percent indirect cost rate
Grant Total	$231,800	

Note: Amounts are for example only and do not reflect an existing budget.

simple computer spreadsheet or, in some districts, with a report from the accounting software. At least monthly, the change leader should check expenses to ensure, first, that the money is being used in the way that was intended, and second, that the money is being used at all. The problem with accounting for the federal funds separately is that the district may forget that those funds are available. Some grants have limited carryover provisions, and some have no carryover provisions, so it is a wise idea to expend all of the grant funds in each grant year. Table 3.3 shows the same Title I grant at midyear with the expenses that have occurred to date. Following it is a list of questions that the change leader must answer or find the answer to. The school business office is the first place to start in the search for answers to these questions.

Looking at this midyear report, the change leader must ask some questions in his or her assessment of the progress of the grant at midyear:

Salaries: At midyear, salaries should be about one half expended. Professional staff is higher than one half expended and nonprofessional staff is lower. Why? Will there be money enough to pay salaries through the year? The salary amount will vary as you identify the salaries of the particular individuals paid by the grant. This may be such a salary variation. Check with the business office to confirm this.

Equipment: The technology equipment line is almost totally expended, but the nontechnology line isn't. Was furniture obtained from the district's storerooms? Was the furniture purchased? Furniture and

Table 3.3.   Midgrant Report of Expenditures

Budget Description	Budgeted Amount	Expenditures as of January 31, 20XX	Amount Remaining
Professional Staff	$80,000.00	$42,701.00	$37,299.00
Support Staff	$64,000.00	$29,083.00	$34,917.00
Equipment			
(Nontechnology)	$1,000.00	$997.00	$3.00
Equipment (Technology)	$10,000.00	$9,827.00	$173.00
Purchased Services	$0.00	$50.00	$(50.00)*
Supplies and Materials	$29,210.00	$21,094.50	$8,115.50
Travel	$0.00	$0.00	$0.00
Benefits	$36,000.00	$17,946.00	$18,054.00
Indirect Costs	$11,590.00	$0.00	$11,590.00
Grant Total	$231,800.00	$121,699.00	$110,101.50

Note: Amounts are for example only and do not reflect an existing budget.
*A number in parentheses denotes a negative number.

supply money should be spent early in the school year in order to get the maximum benefit. If a large amount of this money is not expended by midyear, this raises questions about the status of the program. The change leader will need to check into that.

Purchased services: This shows an expense that was not planned. What was it for? This may require that the district apply for a budget adjustment from the government. Check with your district business administrator when there are changes like this to ensure that all forms are filed properly.

Supplies and materials: There is potential available money here. Were all the supplies purchased that were planned?

Benefits: These are in line with the salary changes.

Indirect costs: Why is nothing expended here? This is because districts generally take indirect costs from a grant only once, at the end of the year.

After looking at the numbers and answering the questions, the change leader can then modify spending patterns if necessary, or apply for grant amendments. Generally, a 10 percent variation in a budget line is allowed without filing a budget amendment, but if you think that you need to move a large amount of money, a budget amendment is always advisable.

After the grant year is over, the district will need to file a final report that will show exactly what was spent from the grant. The district will not receive more than was allotted, even if more was spent. This final report will identify positions that Title moneys funded, as well as asking for proof of other expenditures.

There is a commonly used business office term that must be explained here for the change leader before discussion about final reporting for grants. That is the word *charged*. In referring to the final report of grants this term will be used in the context of assigning an expense to a grant. If a purchase or a salary is charged to a grant, that means that the money for the expense is taken from that grant's funds. Because the change leader's district may be dealing with multiple grants, it is very important that expenses be charged to the correct grant to maximize the use of funds and ensure accuracy of reporting.

Professional staff and nonprofessional staff salaries may have to be reported by the name of the staff member as well as the percentage of his or her salary that is paid for by the Title funds in question. Therefore the change leader will need to be aware of names, positions, yearly salaries, and the percentage of time paid for by these funds, so that the change leader will be able to document, for instance, that John Doe is an elementary reading specialist who earns an average salary of forty-five thousand dollars. John is paid 40 percent from Title I funds, so eighteen thousand dollars of his salary is credited to the grant. Staff members may be charged to more than one grant, but never in excess of their yearly salary, and never in excess of 100 percent. If John Doe is charged 40 percent to Title I, he may also be charged a percentage to Title V or Title II-D, up to 100 percent of his salary. If Mr. Doe's salary is charged completely to grants, then his salary should not appear in the general fund budget at all.

Benefits must be in line with the amount of a salary that is paid from the grant. The change leader cannot pay a part of a staff member's salary from a grant, but charge all of the benefits to the grant. Make sure that the amount of benefits charged can be documented. For instance, if 40 percent of the salary is charged to a grant, only 40 percent of medical insurance is charged there. Do not charge Social Security in excess of the salary that is charged to the grant in question.

For purchased services the change leader may be required to identify the vendor and the type of service. The contract for the service should be on file in the district simply as a good accountability practice, but in the case of federal moneys, the government may require a copy also. The change leader must have easy access to that contract.

Technology equipment may require preapproval of the purchase. If the initial grant application denied the use of funds for technology, the reporting of expenses for technology may be problematic for the change leader. The change leader must keep in mind any changes to the proposed budget that the government may have made in the approval process.

For nontechnology equipment and supplies and materials, the change leader will be required to identify the vendor, the invoice or purchase order number, or the check number that paid for the purchase. In some states copies of the invoices may be required. It is necessary to have access to all of this data.

For travel, the reason for the travel and the staff member involved must be identified. Again, one must have documentation available in the event that there are questions. A grant can only be used to pay for travel if the staff member is doing work associated with the grant. For instance, Title I funds may not normally be used to send a teacher of the gifted and talented to a conference.

The expense for indirect costs cannot exceed the amount that has previously been approved with the Consolidated Application, and that is a flat percentage of the expenses for the grant. Individual states may have varying regulations as to the expenses that may be included for calculation of the indirect costs.

There will be a form that must be completed for the final expenditure report for each grant. If the change leader has access to information, and that information has been maintained during the grant year, it is not an onerous task to fill out the final expenditure form.

MONITORING ENTITLEMENT GRANTS

It is important for the change leader to be cognizant of what is happening in the federal grants that he or she is monitoring. Regulations may be modified on a yearly basis, but more than that, the change leader must be aware of the grants on a day-to-day basis, particularly large grants like Title I.

In the area of use of funds the change leader must know that an entitlement grant is like a minifund in accounting that must be maintained and monitored separately. The budget for the grant must not be used solely in filing and then deposited in a desk drawer until the time for final filing. The budget for the grant must be a living document and should be consulted whenever an expenditure is made, in the same way that a general fund budget is consulted. If the budget is not consulted on a regular basis the change leader will have a much more difficult time with filing the final expenditure report.

The change leader must know the beginning date and the ending date of each grant since not all dates are the same. Some grant years may be from July 1 to June 30, yet others may be from September 1 to August 31. In order to qualify as a valid expense for a grant, the expense must occur within the grant year, and the expense must be documented as having occurred during the grant year.

For the change leader, this means that orders must not be placed prior to the start of the grant year. All educators understand that there must be supplies to open a program, so the change leader should cooperate with the school district to ensure that these beginning supplies are in place. Copy paper and office supplies can be ordered from the grant funds at a later date. Books may already be available in another program within the district. The change leader does not need to start the grant year with a substandard program. In the case of entitlements, however, since these have been in place for many years, the change leader will undoubtedly have some materials and supplies remaining from the previous year so that the entitlement grant programs continue unimpeded in the next grant year.

Additionally, to ensure that expenses occur within the grant year, the change leader must not wait until the end of the grant year to expend money, as sometimes occurs. When orders are placed late in the grant year there may not be sufficient time for the vendor to process the order and the district to pay for the order within the grant year. It is not the date of the order that counts as a grant expense, but the date of the payment. Therefore, at two months before the end of the grant year, all purchases of supplies and materials should be complete in order to allow for sufficient processing time.

FEDERAL AUDITS

From time to time the federal government will choose to audit a district's federal program. This audit may be strictly random, or it may be triggered by what the government has seen on filings from the school district. These federal audits are significant in that a negative audit can reduce or eliminate the amount of entitlement funds that the district receives.

To avoid triggering a federal audit, there are some things that the change leader can do:

First, make sure to meet all filing deadlines for the initial application, the final report, and any intermediate filings that are required. Some grants will have quarterly filings required or some districts may choose to file more frequently in order to receive payment on a more regular basis. Also, when a district chooses to change its use of funds from what was submitted in the initial application, an amendment must be filed in a timely manner.

Second, monitor grants closely. In the finance area the accounting must be accurate. Expenses must be charged to the correct grant and the change leader must ensure that initial and final reporting figures on the financial reports are not so widely disparate as to cause concern. Amendments, of course, will alleviate that concern. In the area of programs, the change leader must ensure that the grant money is used for the purposes specified by the grant.

Third, maintain the records that are necessary to document expenses and personnel. The school district business and personnel offices should have these records on file for the change leader so that there is access to them.

To survive a federal audit, the district will be required to produce documentation for any and all expenses associated with any and all grants. The best attitude for the district and the change leader to take is to be helpful and cooperative in answering questions and in producing information that is requested. When the audit is complete there may be suggestions from the government as to ways that the district should improve in its management of grants. It is important to heed those suggestions and change practices and procedures accordingly.

SUMMARY

Clearly the mandates and the regulations of No Child Left Behind are a double-edged sword for the school district. On the one hand the change leader now has a government that seems as eager as he or she is to improve education. But on the other hand, there is a myriad of new timelines and deadlines that the school districts have to meet in order to avoid sanctions.

The reauthorization of ESEA (the Elementary and Secondary Education Act) brought with it the new regulations of No Child Left Behind: highly qualified staff members, demonstration of Adequate Yearly Progress, and sanctions against schools and districts that do not meet deadlines or that are determined to be persistently dangerous.

Those sanctions can even go so far as to require a school district to send its own students to other school districts.

Application for ESEA funds requires completion of the Consolidated Application, which contains a narrative, information on student demographics, and a proposed budget for each of the grants for which the district is eligible. It is a process that requires time and careful attention. The budget that is submitted with the Consolidated Application becomes the budget for the grant with which it is included.

The change leader should focus the use of the entitlement grants to receive the maximum monetary support for the reform the school district has designated. Programs that are not effective should not be continued just because they have "always been there" or because federal funds support the programs. Programs supported by federal funds must be those that are effective in moving toward the goal of reform. In deciding which programs to use, the change leader must be aware of the issue of supplement versus supplant as it applies to the use of federal funds.

The change leader must build trust with all constituencies of the school district by using the federal funds as effectively and as wisely as possible. It will be necessary for the change leader to know and to monitor the budgets of each of the ESEA grants in order to ensure that this occurs. The money for the federal grants should of course be accounted for separately to maintain this accountability. The change leader must also ensure that all filing deadlines are met, lest the untimely filing trigger a federal audit of funds flowing into the school district.

The only option that remains for a school district that does not wish to be subject to the regulations of No Child Left Behind is to refuse federal funds. This is not an option that many school districts are able to choose; therefore school districts must operate within the mandates of NCLB.

CHAPTER 4

A Taxing Problem for Schools: Property Taxes

Using property taxes to fund education has a long tradition in America but, nevertheless, it seems that no one likes to pay taxes, no matter what income level he or she has. The adage that states that nothing is certain in life except death and taxes is certainly a truism applicable to this chapter. A citizen does not have a choice about paying taxes; it is a "given" of daily life in this country. It is possible, though, that taxes may be easier for taxpayers to accept if those taxpayers can see what services they are receiving from that tax money. Nearly every person knows someone who is receiving Social Security or Medicare; the benefit is visible and tangible; services are received. When there is a war, the citizens see the armed forces and all their matériel go off to defend the country, and can follow the progress of the war (and the use of their tax dollars) in the media. A resident of a municipality gets running water and uses sewers and roads maintained by taxes paid to that municipality. In many areas, taxpayers can see how their tax money is being spent on a tangible service. But then those same citizens are required to pay school taxes, and the challenges for the change leader begin.

State aid is seen as the state's money. Federal entitlement grants are seen as the federal government's money. Property taxes, however, are seen in much more individual terms. Each taxpayer pays money based on his or her own property. The taxpayer writes a check to pay these school taxes or sees the charge for school taxes on his or her mortgage statement. School taxes are used to support the schools in the municipality; the taxpayer may know staff members, students, or school board members. For all of these reasons, school property taxes are a very personal issue to a taxpayer.

In addition to being a very personal issue, education is not something tangible or visible that a citizen can experience, like running water or a doctor visit paid for by Medicare. Education is something that the society does for its children and for the future; there is not an immediate result. Educators know that education is a long-term investment, but not all members of the public realize that, nor is this a society that waits patiently for results. As a culture, we expect immediate results or tangible proof of benefit. Some would attribute this cultural impatience to the pervasive influence of the media, where problems are solved on television in thirty to sixty minutes and news is given in headlines only.

The problem with visibility of education is twofold. First, what the taxpayer frequently "sees" are only the negative aspects of education. Right now the taxpayer "sees" news stories that tell of how American schools are lagging behind other industrialized nations in measures of achievement. The taxpayer "sees" sometimes-outlandish clothing styles that are a product of the broader culture, but blames the schools for not training children better. The taxpayer "sees" a rising school tax bill. What the taxpayer cannot "see" is the intangibles of education. The taxpayer cannot "see" that in twenty years the student with all the body piercings may be the CEO of a computer company contributing to the health of the economy. The taxpayer cannot "see" what a student's life would be like without an education. No one can guarantee those things. Truly, education and educators are selling an intangible product.

The change leader will be confronted with objections from the taxpayers that are the same from district to district and from state to state: that too many nonessential things are being taught in the schools (and paid for by tax dollars); that some citizens have no children, so they object to paying for education; or that the tax money is not being spent effectively. Every educator has heard those arguments. It is the job of the change leader to refute the arguments, to educate the public about education, and to create support for reform. No longer can education and the educational system go its own way without regard to the public opinion of the community. If a change leader tries to make change without community support, the change is doomed to failure.

HOW IS SCHOOL PROPERTY TAX DETERMINED?

Naturally, every state has its own specific modifications to the general method for determining the exact tax rate to be charged in a municipality. This section of the chapter will give brief overviews of what the main components are that go into determining a tax rate. The change leader will probably not be directly involved in the calculation of the tax rate, but he or she will have to be familiar with the terms that are involved.

When referring to property taxes, a *taxpayer* is a property owner whose property lies within the boundary of a school district. If a person does not own property, he or she does not directly pay property taxes to the school district. If a person is renting or leasing a home, apartment, or property, the charge for the cost of school property taxes will be reflected, no doubt, in the amount of the rent or the lease that is paid. However, a renter is not a property taxpayer in the usual sense of the word.

Assessment is simply the assignment of a value to a property as decided by the official *assessor* of the municipality. The *assessor's office* will look at a property and decide on the value of the property, called the *assessed value* of a property. This is the figure that appears on tax bills. In some districts the assessed value will be a number that is very close to *market value* or the price for which the property could be sold on the open real estate market. The term *property value* is used interchangeably with assessed value.

One problem with property taxes that the change leader may encounter is that commercial properties and residential properties may be assessed differently in a given municipality. While this is a problem for the assessors to deal with, the change leader will want to be aware of this. When citizens question taxes, the issue of perceived fairness is one of the foremost concerns. When a change leader is seeking support from the public, he or she may well be confronted with the question "Is it fair that businesses pay more?" Be prepared to acknowledge, if not address, that concern. Talk to the school district business office for information, or talk to the municipality's assessor. Refer concerned business owners to the appropriate office where these concerns can be addressed. The school district itself has no control over this, but can offer information to the business owner. Some municipalities follow a plan of regular reassessment that results in assessed values being closer to market values. Concerns and misunderstandings on the part of the public are more likely to occur when the assessed value is significantly different from the market value of the property, as illustrated in the next paragraph.

In some municipalities, however, the assessor uses a percentage of market value to determine assessment. To illustrate this, in a municipality that uses full assessment or 100 percent assessment, a house that has a value of two hundred thousand dollars will have a formal assessed value of two hundred thousand dollars. If that municipality had a 50 percent assessment, the same property would have an assessed value of one hundred thousand dollars. If the municipality had a 10 percent assessment, that property would have an assessed value of twenty thousand dollars. Obviously this can cause questions when the property owner knows that homes in his or her neighborhood sell for two hundred thousand dollars, but his or her property's assessed value is significantly less. This is another issue that is not under the control of the change leader, but of which the change leader needs to be aware.

The *tax levy* is the amount of money that the school district needs to collect from the taxpayers of the school district to support its programs. To determine the tax levy, the school district prepares a budget of all proposed expenditures for the next fiscal year. District officials then prepare an estimate of all of the possible revenues that the district will receive. These revenues can be from state aid, federal entitlement grants, bank interest, admissions to athletic contests, and so forth. The amount of estimated nontax revenue is subtracted from the amount of total expenditures, and the remainder of the money needed becomes the tax levy.

The tax levy is the part of the schools' revenue over which the district has the greatest amount of control. Federal entitlements are a set figure, and are restricted in their use. State aid can be estimated closely, if one is familiar with the formulas, but the change leader can affect the amount received only within the parameters of those formulas. Since other sources of revenue are more or less fixed, the effective use of district money has a direct impact on the tax levy. If expenses in a proposed budget are decreased, the tax levy decreases also. If the expenses in a budget increase, the tax levy increases. The district can have a direct impact on the amount of money to be collected from the local tax-payer. This is one of the reasons why it is important for the school district to be effective and accountable in spending these tax dollars.

The *tax rate* is the amount of money that a property owner will have to pay for each one thousand dollars of value of the property. The tax rate is calculated in two steps. First one divides the entire amount of property assessment for the school district by one thousand. This is because the tax rate is expressed in terms of dollars per thousand of *valuation* (the value of the property assigned by the assessor's office). The second step is to divide the amount of the tax levy by the amount of assessed value in the school district.

As an example, assume that there is a school district that wants to collect ten million dollars in property taxes from the community of the school district. Assume also that the school district has four hundred million dollars in property value. The calculation of the property tax rate appears in table 4.1.

Therefore, the tax rate for this imaginary school district is twenty-five dollars per thousand of property value.

To determine the school tax amount for a given property is easy to do. Simply divide the assessed value of the property by 1,000 and multiply that figure by the tax rate. A property in this school district that has an assessed value of $100,000 will have a school tax of $2,500. A property that is assessed at $200,000 will have a school tax of $5,000. See the calculation in table 4.2.

This final amount is the figure that appears on the property owner's tax bill from the school district.

COLLECTION OF TAXES

In some areas, the school district actually collects its own taxes from the property owners of the community. This makes the payment of the

Table 4.1.   Calculation of School District Tax Rate

Total Property Value	$400,000,000.00
Total Property Value Divided by 1,000	$400,000.00
Tax Levy	$10,000,000.00
Tax Rate	
(the tax levy divided by total property value divided by 1,000)	$25.00

Note: Amounts are for example only and do not reflect an existing budget.

Table 4.2.   Calculation of Tax Rate on Individual Properties

	$100,000.00	$200,000.00
Property Value	$100,000.00	$200,000.00
Divide by 1,000	100.00	200.00
Tax rate	$25.00	$25.00
Multiply the property value		
divided by 1,000 by the tax rate	$2,500.00	$5,000.00

Note: Amounts are for example only and do not reflect an existing budget.

school tax a very visible and defined act. That means that property owners are more aware of the school tax than if the payment were a part of the larger tax bill from the municipality. Taxpayers who are more aware of the tax payment may have more questions. If the school tax is a part of a larger municipal bill that goes out to property owners, the municipality then transmits the money to the school district. Some districts may have one tax payment per year, others two or more. Variations are myriad and are specific to the particular municipality. A confirmation of a local process may be obtained at the local assessor's office or the school district business office.

VOTING ON TAXES

Taxes are everywhere. There are federal income, state income, sales, Social Security, village property, county property, estate, and transfer taxes (the list goes on and on), as well as the property tax for the school district. Taxes are compulsory in that the taxpayer does not have the option of deciding whether or not to pay the tax, nor does he or she have the opportunity to decide the rate of the tax—except, of course, in the matter of the school district property tax.

In most school districts, taxpayers become voters as well. The residents of the municipality have an opportunity to vote yea or nay on the school district budget, and, therefore, on the tax the school district levies on the taxpayers. Congress does not ask the voters to approve its budget each year, and neither do the state legislatures. Governments regularly carry out projects that voters and taxpayers may object to, projects that would not be granted funding if put to a vote like the school district budget. To express their objection to a tax policy, taxpayers can lobby and vote individual members out of office, but the process of doing so is long, and the effect of doing so is not immediate. The state and federal governments are simply too large for taxpayers to have that kind of impact.

Even in cities and villages, taxpayers can seldom do more than make their opinions known and vote out incumbents who do not behave in a fashion with which the taxpayers agree. In a small governmental division, though, it may be easier to make oneself heard, or to lobby incumbents.

In districts where taxpayers vote on the school budget, the school district presents a budget to the taxpayers and actually asks the taxpayers to vote on that budget. In essence, the school district does what no other governmental body does: it asks approval for how the taxpayers' money should be spent. This is the one opportunity for the taxpayer to say yes or no to a taxation plan. It is unfortunate, but true, that taxpayers who feel animosity toward the federal, state, or city government and its tax spending plan may direct it all toward the school budget because this is the one opportunity to say no. The taxpayer may object to subsidies from the federal government, but can't say no there, so may say no to the school district. The taxpayer may be dissatisfied with garbage pickup or road maintenance of the city, but may release that anger by saying no to the school district. Or, the taxpayer could be honestly against the school district budget for the reason that the education being provided is not adequate, so he or she may say no to the school district budget. While all of these different motivations result in the same outcome, a "no" for the school budget, it is the job of the school district to understand why the "no" votes occur. Then the process for the school district becomes one of education.

When referring to votes on taxes, however, the change leader must remember that not all of the people who will be voting on the school budget are taxpayers. The taxpayers who vote are the people who own property and live within the school district. Those who rent or lease and who live in the district are eligible to vote, but may not be paying school taxes directly. This means that, when educating the public regarding taxes, the change leader will be talking to taxpayers and nontaxpayers alike.

EDUCATING THE PUBLIC ABOUT TAXES

Above all else, the district must be offering a quality educational program in order to secure support from the public in regard to property taxes. People generally do not mind paying for something if they are receiving a quality product. If the program that the school district offers is not of a high quality, then this is where the change leader becomes very important. If there is not already a quality program in place, the change leader must be able to present a plan for how the school district is going to change the existing program into one that is effective and is of a high quality. But the change leader should never make the mistake of simply offering a plan that cannot or will not be carried out, because when the next year's budget vote arrives, taxpayers will want to see the results of the promise and assurances from the previous year. If the change leader cannot show that things have changed in any way, the support for the school budget will diminish rapidly.

In educating the public about taxes, the change leader must be willing to acknowledge the validity of some of the taxpayers' feelings. Yes, some people may feel that their taxes are too high because of their assessment, so tell them to whom or to which municipal office to take that problem. Yes, some people may object to the tax rate, so the district must be able to clearly explain how the number was derived. Yes, some people may feel unfairly burdened by taxes, but the change leader may feel that way also. In terms of being unable to have any input in the spending proclivities of large municipal organizations, the taxpayers of the school district and the change leader are in the same circumstance: they pay what they are told. Help the taxpayers feel that the school district is not the enemy. Start by using those skills outlined in chapter 1.

Make sure that the money that is collected in taxes is used in the most effective ways possible. The change leader must be able to speak to this issue for the public. Taxpayers will want to be assured that the purchasing process of the school district has been used to get the best price for goods and services. If there is visible waste or if there is even the intimation of cronyism in awarding contracts, the public will mistrust the district and the words of the change leader. The other aspect of effectiveness that will have to be presented is in the area of curriculum.

Were the programs that tax dollars paid for effective in raising student test scores?

Taxpayers will want the district to be accountable for the money that has been spent. All of the skills in presenting budgets, giving interim financial reports, and reporting on final expenditures must be put to use here. Because a property tax is local, members of the public feel a greater investment in the use of the money. The taxpayer can see the tax money going out from his or her checking account and into that of the school district. It is a much more personal feeling of investment than trying to watch one's money move through the federal government because the federal government is simply too large.

Use all of the recommended accounting skills in chapters 2 and 3 to ensure that accountability and to facilitate the tracking and the administration of expense. Remember that more accurate financial data can provide better control of expenses for the change leader, the district business administrator, and the school district. In addition, taxpayers will be able to feel confident that proper procedures are being used.

The change leader will find another unique aspect with the issue of property taxes. This is that it seems easier for a taxpayer to understand, or question, an expense of two thousand dollars or two hundred dollars as opposed to an expense of two million or two billion dollars. This is logical. All people respond to issues based on their own personal experience. Because most taxpayers, and educators, have more experience with a smaller expense, discussion of school district expenses will have more meaning to the taxpayer than discussion of national expenses. Most people can relate to the consequences of a two thousand dollar expense, but half a million dollars in expense may be beyond experience and comprehension.

Give hard data when educating the public. Show them the actual budget numbers and tell them how the numbers were decided upon. Be able to tell the taxpayers specifically what programs these numbers contain. A taxpayer will be more likely to support the budget based on statements like, "This expense of forty thousand dollars is earmarked for a program developed by XYZ company to improve reading scores in the fourth grade. This program has proved successful in ten other districts with exactly our demographics in this state," as opposed to, "This forty thousand dollars is earmarked for a summer program."

Answer all the public's questions clearly and simply. The change leader may not even be aware that it is happening, but one must not lapse into educational or financial jargon. Even though the educators and the district business administrator may understand what the change leader is saying, the taxpayer who has no experience with either of these subjects will not understand. As an example, the change leader may dismiss as untrustworthy political statements that seem to support opposing views in the same statement or that are circuitous or unclear. In that same way, the taxpayer will dismiss statements of the school district that are not understandable and clear.

In educating the public, the district must never try to "spin" information. Refer to the example from chapter 1 regarding the way to "spin" the announcement of unsatisfactory test scores. How will a taxpayer feel if he or she hears from that particular "spin" that test scores are at an acceptable level in the district, yet does not know of any students among all his or her friends' children who are doing well? The taxpayer will feel betrayed, or that the school district is simply carrying on business the same way that the other governments do. Trust will be gone. It is not fair, but it is a fact, that because school districts deal with children, we are held to a higher standard, one where we are expected to be more honest, more moral, more dedicated, and more altruistic than other governmental bodies.

Find someone who is able to clearly explain the formula and the basis for calculating the local property tax. Have that person educate your taxpayers so that they understand where that tax number came from.

Try to get a wider sampling of the taxpaying community involved. It is a truism that the people who are dissatisfied with a situation are more likely to get involved than if they were satisfied. Reach out to the parents who are satisfied with the education in the schools and have them speak at public meetings. Have parents write editorials; those who are working against a school budget certainly will. Have businesspeople in the community who are pleased with the schools talk to other businesspeople. Community members who are pleased with the outcomes of the schools can do a great deal to educate other members of the community.

FOCUS THE USE OF TAX MONEY

Effectiveness and accountability always come back to the issue of focus. Taxpayers won't mind (as much) paying taxes to receive a quality
educational program. Perform the needs assessment that is required,
and identify the reform needed. Then use the money received in tax
collections to further that reform. The district should not use tax money
(or any money, for that matter) to fund a program that is not effective
in increasing student achievement. Everything that has been said about
the importance of focus in all other chapters is equally applicable here.
The difference is that a local taxpayer is much more personally involved in his or her local property taxes than in other taxes.

SUMMARY

Property taxes for the support of a school district are a very personal issue for the taxpayer, being based on the value of the individual's home.
In addition, the property taxes that pay for education are paying for a
service that each individual taxpayer may not directly use: an investment in the future. The job of the change leader is to help the taxpayers see what they are receiving from the schools for their tax dollars.

Once again the focus or the use of the money is paramount. If a
school district makes good use of tax dollars, if achievement increases
and schools are safe and effective, the district will have fewer com-
plaints and concerns with taxpayers. If, however, achievement is poor
and the schools are seen as dangerous, there will be more issues with
taxpayers. Taxpayers want to see, or at least to feel, that the tax money
that they *must* pay is being put to good use.

CHAPTER 5

Competitive Grants:
Can They Grant Educational Reform?

An Internet search will reveal a plethora of books that have been written on the subject of how to write grants and the rules to follow to ensure the greatest likelihood of securing a grant. Since there is so much information that is available to the change leader on the subject of writing competitive grants, this chapter will be brief. The goal of this chapter is to make the change leader aware of resources and possibilities in applying for these grants, to alert the change leader to the unique negatives and positives of competitive grants, and to remind the change leader (as every chapter does) to focus consideration of competitive grants on the vision of educational reform in the school district.

WHAT IS A COMPETITIVE GRANT?

In chapter 3 this book talked about federal entitlement grants. The funds from these grants are allotted to districts by virtue of legislation and student need; there is not a way for the district to increase the amount of money received. With a competitive grant, however, the district will have more opportunity to influence the amount of money through the application process.

In a competitive grant situation the school district will file an application with the granting authority. Then the school district competes against all of the other entities that are applying for money from the grantor. Since it is probable that not all applicants will receive grant money, the money that is given to a school district will depend on the quality of the application. Fortunately, there are a few things that the change leader can do to influence that quality, and these things will be mentioned later in this chapter.

WHERE DO COMPETITIVE GRANTS COME FROM?

Competitive grants come from a variety of sources. Governments are one source. Both the federal government and state governments have grants that a school district can apply for. Some of these grant applications may be as simple as contacting a legislator and making a request. Others may require formal applications. For instance, the 21st Century Learning Communities grants require extensive application and collaboration with other constituencies. In applying for a competitive federal grant, the change leader should follow the same practices that he or she uses in seeking a competitive grant from a nongovernmental source.

In seeking additional governmental funds it is always wise to contact the state and federal legislators for guidance and assistance. Legislators want to be able to direct federal and state funds to the area that they represent and can sometimes help in guiding the change leader. A legislator can direct the change leader to the source of the money, can direct the change leader to the appropriate person for assistance, or perhaps can proffer the grant himself or herself. In some cases legislators are allocated a certain amount of funds that can be freely distributed to their representative area.

Local governments may also have programs that will offer grants to school districts. Because this is local government these grants may be easier to obtain, but there will probably be a smaller amount of money attached to the grant.

Competitive grants can come from corporations and other businesses. The change leader should explore that possibility with local businesses as well as with the multinational corporations.

Nonprofit foundations can also be a source of competitive grants. These foundations can be small, local foundations or national groups.

In other words, a competitive grant can be sought in many venues, and an Internet search will produce a long list of potential sources. There are grant newsletters that will alert grant seekers when a new grant program is announced, or, for the change leader who does not have the time to invest, there are people who earn their living seeking grants for entities. A competitive grant is a definite possibility for funding educational reform, but not one that can be relied upon as a steady, yearly source of income. Some administrators, in creating a proposed budget, will include competitive grants as a revenue. Unless these grants have already been awarded to the school district, it is not a good idea to include them. This will give the district a false sense of the amount of revenue that it will have and it can lead to overspending.

FOCUS AND COMPETITIVE GRANTS

In writing a grant, remember what your focus is in the school district.

If there is a negative side to competitive grants it is that the granting entity may have its own focus for the use of the grant, and that focus may not align with the focus toward educational reform that the school district and the change leader hold. If the grant money has to be used for a specific purpose, one that detracts from the reform vision of the district, this is not a grant that the district wants to seek, to accept, or to use. Of course, it is always difficult for a school district to turn down money. There are greater needs than there are resources in schools today, but the district and the change leader need to remain focused on what must be accomplished for the students.

Rather than being reactive and simply accepting money that is given, the change leader should actively seek grant money where the purpose of the grant is the same as the reform focus of the district. In the same way that the change leader can focus use of entitlement grants to support a reform, he or she can use competitive grants to fund reform.

APPLYING FOR A COMPETITIVE GRANT

The change leader will have experienced this many times in his or her career: someone in the district has an idea for a new program, and his or her solution for funding it is, "We'll just write a grant." If only it were that easy.

Applications for a competitive grant can be extensive. A grant may require participation and concurrence by groups other than the school district. This will require planning and coordination with those groups. A program may need to be detailed in writing for the grant. Certainly a budget and justification for the amount of money sought will need to be provided. It is clear that there is an investment of time that is necessary for application for a grant.

In order to provide the time necessary to apply for competitive grants some districts employ one or more grant writers whose job is to seek additional funds. A grant writer may be a part of the district staff, perhaps with additional duties, or a grant writer's services may be contracted. Grant writers who are part of the district staff receive their paycheck from the district and are paid a salary for their work. A contracted grant writer is paid as a vendor for the school district. Grant services may be contracted at a flat rate per grant, or they may be paid as a percentage of the grant money received. If a grant writer is paid on the basis of a percentage of money received, there is no payment if a grant is not received. There are, of course, combinations of staff and contracted grant writing that will vary with the district involved. The change leader should know that there are services available to assist in the writing of grant applications.

When applying for a grant it is important for the change leader to know that creativity and novelty may not be viewed as a positive. First of all, the application for the grant will ask the applicant for certain information. The change leader must give that information completely, but not include extraneous details. The application might request that the information be in a certain format. If it does, the change leader should adhere to that format. The specification of type of information and format is for the use of the grantors in deciding between applicants. It is much easier to decide if information and format are the same.

With a competitive grant, the change leader may be required to include base data for a pre- and postgrant evaluation. This requires that the data be available in a student accountability system. The change leader must also ensure that records are kept in that accountability system for comparison at the end of the grant.

Because entitlement grants are well established, it is easy for the change leader to establish a timeline for applying for, monitoring, and reporting for these funds. Competitive grants are not as dependable in terms of timelines. A competitive grant may give the change leader thirty days for application. This requires a rapid response in terms of gathering information and writing the application.

MONITORING COMPETITIVE GRANTS

Each grant that the district receives will have its own guidelines for filing requirements, yet the same principles that apply to the monitoring of entitlement grants will apply to monitoring competitive grants.

The accounting must be accurate. While the purpose of the grant funds should be the same as the purpose of the district's educational reform, the actual funds must be accounted for separately. Expenses from the grant should be documented and records maintained. Proper procedures must be followed. At the completion of the grant the change leader may be required to produce that documentation, and one does not want to have to re-create records.

An additional issue for the district to monitor is that the grant could span multiple years, and certainly will not necessarily adhere to the timeline used in the federal entitlement grants. Therefore the change leader must be very cognizant of timelines for a competitive grant. Grants crossing fiscal years or remaining in place for multiple years are also a concern for the business office of the school district. If a grant is for multiple years the importance of budgeting becomes paramount. If the change leader wishes the program to be fully funded for those multiple years, he or she must be judicious in his or her use of the grant funds in order to preserve that funding for the longer time period.

The change leader must also be aware of the timeline for a grant because of the rules for expenditures. Grants normally do not allow expenditures that are made before the grant is awarded, or after the grant has expired. The change leader will need to be cognizant of these rules. In any case, it is never a good idea to spend money based on the reception of a competitive grant until that money has been awarded to the school district. It is very tempting, when one is certain that the district will receive a competitive grant, to begin preparing beforehand by purchasing materials needed. Do not do this! If it should happen that the grant is not awarded to the school district, the district's general fund or other grants will have to be used to cover the expense. Money that was earmarked for one certain program will have to be diverted. When dealing with competitive grants it is best for the change leader to be cautious.

All of the effective skills that the change leader must use in managing moneys from the general fund must also be used in managing funds from competitive grants.

SUMMARY

There is a great deal of information that exists on the subject of successful grant writing. The purpose of this chapter is to make the change leader aware of the fact that competitive grants exist and can be used to fund educational reform.

Applying for a competitive grant can be a time-consuming process for the change leader. If the time is not available for such application, the school district may hire a grant writer specifically to seek out this type of funding. A grant writer can be a staff member, or can work as a vendor for the school district.

All of the skills that are used in effective administration of federal, state, and local moneys must also be used in monitoring competitive grants. The organization that grants the school district money will be expecting integrity, accountability in financing and programs, focus on the stated goal of the grant, and communication with the grantor. The change leader will need to use the skills of decentralized decision making to help the grant run at its most effective.

CHAPTER 6

Using Local Options to
Fund Educational Reform

The change leader who depends on state, federal, and local municipalities as the only source of funds for the support of educational reform may be disappointed in those sources. Previous chapters have shown how funding formulas may restrict the amount of money that is available to be channeled to reform by controlling uses of the money. Competitive grants and entitlement grants can provide alternative avenues for the change leader to acquire additional funds, but there are also ways to involve local community members in supporting educational reform in their own district. Some of the ways of providing additional local dollars can result in a large amount of money coming into the district to support education and its reform. Others may result in only small amounts. Yet others can provide time and services. As with other forms of reform funding, the most important issue is not the amount of money that is available or the amount that is used, but the focus of the dollars, and how that money is put to use for maximum effect. The dollars and the efforts from these local sources need to be focused toward achieving the reform of education in the district according to the needs assessment of the district.

This chapter will talk about some of the most common local ways to increase funding. One local funding method that will be addressed in this chapter is the formation of an educational foundation. This chapter will also address business partnerships with schools, internship and apprenticeship programs, fund-raising, and volunteerism. Naturally this is not an exhaustive list of forms of local support for educational reform. A change leader with a good understanding of the school community will be able to think of many more ways for the individual community to support the schools. An important element to keep in mind is that, since each school district is unique, what will work in one school district may not work in the district that is right next door, so the change leader must be sensitive not only to the needs of the students and the school district, but to the needs and mores of the constituencies in the learning community as well.

As with the issue of competitive grant seeking, there are a number of resources that exist that tell a change leader how to start a foundation, establish a business partnership, or conduct successful fund-raising. Therefore this chapter will not include the specific information on how to go about implementing these things. The resources section at the end of the book lists a number of these available resources, however. This chapter is to discuss the issues that the change leader must face in using different forms of local support.

KNOW THE LEARNING COMMUNITY WELL

The first, and imperative, step for the change leader in initiating any formal local educational support effort is to get to know and to understand all of the constituencies that compose the learning community of the district very, very well. It will not be enough for the change leader to know the schools and the various groups within the schools: the unions, parent groups, teachers, administrators, students, support staff, and so on. Since the change leader will be reaching out to the larger community, he or she will need to be well acquainted with the groups that make up that community. This is a step that, if left out, can cause the downfall of a support effort or can prevent the creation or successful start-up of a program.

The Business Community. The business community has a vested interest in the success of the schools. At the very least, businesses need well-educated employees who are able to read, write, do basic math, and think critically. Right now, in many geographic areas, there is a shortage of these well-educated employment candidates, and businesses cannot find a sufficient number of employees who are trained to the level that is needed. Instead the businesses have to invest sometimes-limited capital not only in training new employees but also in offering remediation to educate employees to the level that they need to begin their jobs.

No longer does an employee stand at a machine, engaged in repetitive actions, making "widgets" (or other manufactured items) for eight hours a day. America is now a technological society that requires employees with more skills at every level. Nowadays even if an employee does work in a widget factory, the machine that makes the widgets is probably linked to a computer, so the employee must be comfortable with technology. There will be manuals for using those widget machines and for troubleshooting problems before calling the technical repair employees, so the employee will have to know how to read and comprehend. Many business are run by employee groups, or at least have employee groups that give input. Using this model, today's employee needs to be able to learn about the wider concepts of widget making and to understand the part that his or her own job plays in that. The employee may even be an investor in the widget company through retirement plans or stock options, so must be able to understand some business financials and his or her function in the creation and maintenance of the business. In some companies the employee may have the responsibility to stop the production line of widgets if he or she sees a problem, so he or she has to be capable of evaluation and be able to take initiative.

To graduate a student who has the basic capacities to become this type of employee is the job of the schools. This may require reform or expansion of a school district's curriculum to include: critical reading skills, higher-level math skills, the ability to evaluate and make judgments, technology skills, or the ability to work as part of a team. Not only is reform important to and for the students in our schools, but reform is important to the businesses that will employ those students.

Good schools affect the success of the whole community. If the supply of educated workers is good, more businesses will relocate to the community. As more businesses open and evolve, more money flows into the community through purchases and through employment salaries. Businesses will become more valuable and the property value of real estate will remain high as the businesses succeed. Investment in the community, whether in a house or a business, will be a sound investment and will attract additional investors. Clearly, better school systems help the business community, and poor school systems hurt businesses.

The business community of the school district is already supporting the schools of the district through the system of school taxes. The change leader should be prepared to address the questions from the business community about why the businesses should do more than simply pay their taxes. Show the business leaders how the community can benefit from good schools. By and large, since businesspeople understand the value of a sound investment, they will understand the value of investing in the schools. To justify the confidence of the business leaders, however, actual reform will need to take place, and results and outcomes in the schools will need to change. Communication with the business leaders will show them what is being done and help them understand the process. Fiscal accountability will make business members of the community feel secure that their money (investment) is being spent effectively. All of the attributes in chapter 1 that build trust in the school learning community will also build trust in the business community.

The Economic Climate. The change leader must be familiar with the economic status of the community. If a community is in economic straits, the change leader will not be able to expect a great deal of cash money from the businesses, but those same businesses may be willing to provide a different type of support. These businesses could contribute their expertise through training and through the assignment of personnel. Therefore the change leader must be familiar with the types of businesses in the community. Are the jobs in the community primarily in manufacturing? Are the businesses involved in providing technology goods and/or services? Is there a hospital or a university that is a part of the learning community? What are the largest businesses? Various types of businesses will have different skills to contribute to the support of education reform, so the change leader will need to know what skills are available.

If residents within the school district boundaries have high salaries, that might indicate success for a foundation or other monetary form of support, but if the community residents are less affluent, the change leader will need to seek support that involves time and effort for reform, like a volunteer program.

Demographics. The change leader needs to know who the individuals are who make up the community. In order to build support for reform, the change leader will need to show each of the demographic groups how it will benefit from reform of education, and the needs of these groups may be different.

Take for instance the matter of residents who are without children in the schools. If these people are young and are just starting out in their families and careers, good schools will be important to their children as they grow and mature. Are these residents professionals without children? The quality of education given to students in the district will affect the success of the residents' businesses or their professions. If they commute to a different place to work, the quality of life that they have while at home may depend on the quality of the schools. Are these residents retirees who have already been through the school system with their children? In that case, the children who are being educated now will be the adults who are paying the Social Security payments of those retirees. Each group presents a particular set of challenges in determining the successful form of local support.

Another demographic issue that the change leader needs to know about is whether the community comprises primarily one ethnic or religious group. It would be disaster if the change leader chose a method or an activity that offended a large group of people, like serving beef in a large community of Hindus who revere the cow or emphasizing Halloween celebrations in a community where many people choose not to celebrate because of their religious beliefs. A faux pas in this area could lose support for the school rather than garner more.

History. As in so much of education, what has happened in the past will affect what can happen in the future. Have there been any previous efforts by the district to create any of these forms of local funding? How did it go? Was it successful? What was the community's reaction to this effort? Depending on the history of the district there may be naysayers with the message of "We tried that [add a number here] years ago and it didn't work" or traditionalists with the most horrifying educational message of all, "It's always been done that way." Get to know the history of the district and of the community before you set out to implement your strategy.

Concurrent Community Efforts. The change leader should find out what other local efforts for support of various nonprofit groups exist in the community. If a local ambulance corps or volunteer fire company has a successful foundation or fund-raising project already, does the change leader want to add another foundation for the schools? Perhaps, or perhaps not; it will depend on the community. Are there already intern and apprentice programs that exist that the school district can tie into without reinventing the wheel? Again, as has been mentioned in every chapter, if the program exists already, but it does not fit into the district's plan for reform, the change leader should not use it. Just because a program already exists does not mean that it will help the movement to reform the district.

FORMS OF COMMUNITY SUPPORT

It is assumed that the district will have done an extensive needs assessment and decided on the direction for reform. Once the change leader has added to that information the knowledge of the school district learning community, it is time to choose which form of local support the change leader wants to use. Some forms will generate cash money. Others will generate in-kind services or time. All of these can be focused to most effectively support the district's reform.

This chapter will not attempt to offer all of the information regarding how to start educational foundations, business partnerships, and so forth. The change leader can find information on that in books and articles written for that express purpose. The intent of this chapter is, rather, to talk in more general terms about the establishment and the use of those ways of supporting reform as opposed to the more technical aspects. This chapter will also raise questions that the change leader must consider before moving to one of these local methods of funding and proactively warn the change leader about some objections that members of the learning community may raise.

Foundations

A foundation attached to a school district should seek the Internal Revenue Service designation as a 501c(3) corporation. This is the designation of a nonprofit group and it allows the foundation to function without tax implications. This means that the foundation will not have to pay taxes on purchases and that groups or individuals contributing money will be able to take that contribution as a tax deduction. The 501c(3) designation can make a difference in the amount of money a foundation collects. Understandably, both businesses and individuals are more likely to make a donation if it will also function as a tax deduction for them.

A district should consult the Internal Revenue Service and the district's legal counsel in seeking this designation. There is a specific process that must be followed to achieve this designation. The rules for a foundation may differ from those for a school district, in that the foundation may have more freedom in raising money for the school district. For the purpose of the change leader, however, a foundation can be used to raise additional money that will be directed toward reform.

Partnerships

Partnerships between schools and businesses come in as many models as there are partnerships. Each school district with its cooperating businesses creates the model that works for the individual community. The secret, however, of a successful school–business partnership is that both the businesses and the schools are receiving assistance from each other. Put another way, both partners must be receiving a benefit from the partnership arrangement. Partnerships with a business or group of businesses may not result in additional dollars, but can add a great deal to the depth of the learning of the students. A partnership becomes a tool for funding reform when that partnership is built to support the reform.

As with the concept of educational foundations, there is literature available for the change leader that sets out the steps to take in creating the school-business partnership. This chapter is to give the basic information so that the change leader is able to make a decision as to whether pursuit of such a partnership will be in the interest of the school district and its students. Some of the relevant literature is listed in the resources section at the end of this book.

Internships/Apprenticeships

Like partnerships, internships and apprenticeships are a way to fund reform only if focused toward that reform. The change leader must match the needs of the district to the skills taught in the program. For instance, if the reform that is necessary is an increase in technology familiarity and skills, seek internships where the students will learn about repair and use of technology. An internship in woodworking may not address that need. Do not send students to internships that are unrelated to the reform that the district is implementing.

Fund-Raising

There are myriad opportunities for fund-raising. It can be as simple as a candy bar sale and as complex as a black tie dinner event, yet the same basic concepts of fund-raising apply to all such events. Fund-raising can be done by the district itself, a foundation, a parent–teacher organization, or a student club, yet the concerns are the same.

First, if the change leader is planning a fund-raising event, there will undoubtedly be state or district guidelines for what may and may not be done. Even something as simple as a cupcake sale in the school cafeteria will fall under these guidelines. In the case of the cupcake sale, the change leader must know that the federal government prohibits competition with the federal lunch and breakfast program. If a school is involved in the federal lunch program, other groups may not sell food during the time that the federal program is in progress (i.e., during breakfast or lunch times).

Districts may have their own guidelines on what the school district can sell. For instance, some districts will not sell candy because of the alleged links between sugar and hyperactivity. Another district guideline may be regarding the age of students allowed to sell items for the school district. A kindergartener may be cute and irresistible as a salesperson, but there may be concerns regarding safety or propriety. Some districts may not wish students to sell anything at all. Check out the parameters before committing to the event.

If a change leader is to be a good marketer, he or she needs to know the target audience for the sales, so that will require knowledge of the community. Grandma and Grandpa will always buy whatever their grandchild is selling, but to earn as much as possible it is advisable to sell something that the community will want to buy within those parameters of the district policies. One idea that some groups have used is a birthday calendar where people pay to have special dates like birthdays and anniversaries printed on a community calendar. It is something useful that everyone enjoys. These sales have been very successful. Look for fund-raising opportunities that will benefit and involve the community in the schools.

Remember, also, that just because a district has always had an annual greeting card sale or candy drive, it does not mean that these events have to continue, particularly if the amount of sales is going down. The idea in fund-raising is to earn as much money as possible to support the reform.

The change leader must never "overdo" sales. Relatives, neighbors, and parents' coworkers can only buy so many candy bars, cookies, calendars, school district logo cups, stationery sets, lanyards, key chains, and bobble-headed cheerleaders and football quarterbacks before reaching exhaustion. The change leader should carefully choose items to sell and plan the timing carefully. Any selling that the change leader chooses to do will have to mesh with other district efforts, also.

Rather than using only sales of items as a tool for fund-raising, the change leader may wish to explore other events. There is, of course, always the ubiquitous car wash. Sometimes it seems that on any given Saturday, on any main intersection, each corner has its own car wash being held. Districts and groups can use members as service providers and sell other services, too—raking, snow shoveling, and so on—within guidelines and community sensibilities. The change leader may find districts where some parents consider this type of fund-raising to be tantamount to slavery, however. Once again, knowledge of the community is paramount. As mentioned previously, some areas may object to the use of students to provide services, whether it is on the issue of unpaid labor, the issue of safety, or the concern that it is just not proper to use students this way. The change leader who goes against these local mores will fail in his or her attempt to raise funds.

It is always important for a nonprofit organization, like a school district or school foundation, to consider ethics when engaging in any form of fund-raising. When a school district is using students as a vehicle for that fund-raising, the issues of ethics and propriety become even more intense.

In terms of the financial aspect of fund-raising it is essential to maintain complete and accurate accountability for the funds. The change leader must record expenses and revenue, just as if it were the general fund school budget. Do not allow any discrepancies between the two numbers. If it looks like someone is profiting from the event other than the schools, the credibility of the effort will disappear. If the district is selling something, ensure that everyone who has ordered an item receives it. Nearly every person who has supported an educational sales drive has had the experience of ordering a T-shirt, candle, or wrapping paper from an adorable child, but never receiving it. Avoiding this requires precise record keeping on the part of the change leader and all adults involved in the event, and it includes training of the students in ethical business behavior. The event can be a teachable moment.

The school district business office can be a resource for the change leader who is doing fund-raising as regards state guidelines, school district policies, and proper accounting procedures.

Volunteerism

Volunteerism is one of the best ways for the change leader to encourage community members to feel a sense of ownership in the schools. At least a part of the difficulties that school districts encounter in explaining the work of education is that many people have not been inside a school in a long time. It is human nature for community members to believe that schools have remained as they were when these individuals were attending them. Therefore it is easy to dismiss educators' claims about the differences between students today and students from years ago if a person does not know what today's students are like. The knowledge of what schools are like today is necessary before members of the public can adequately understand the implications of and the need for reform.

When people come into a school and can understand what is occurring in a school, they will understand the messages from the school district better, and they will understand the need for reform. Community members who are familiar with the schools will share a common vocabulary with the change leader, so communication will be facilitated. If people feel welcome in the schools, they will see that they are receiving something for their tax dollars, and may not feel so oppressed by school taxes. People who can come into the schools and offer their expertise will feel that they are accomplishing something, will feel that they are a part of the school, and will have ownership in the school and the success of the students.

The problem that some districts find with volunteers is that they have no control over the quality of the skills that the volunteers bring. By definition, volunteers are the people who are willing to serve, but may not be educators, so that is a valid concern. In that case one tactic that the change leader may use is to assign the volunteers to the area where their skills are most effective. Hall monitors need different skills than teachers' aides or library aides. Volunteers in the high school need different skills than volunteers in an elementary school. The change leader should direct the volunteer to the area where his or her skills can be used. Remember that in volunteering, as in employment, if a person feels that his or her skills are not being utilized, he or she will get bored with the position and may not do as good a job, or may simply leave. The change leader who places a volunteer with the same care as an employee will have a happier volunteer and less frustration as the leader of the volunteer program.

Another option that the change leader has is to provide training to the volunteers. For instance, if the district's reading program requires adults to sit and read with children, teach the volunteers what questions to ask, how to assist students, or how much help to give to students. Explain to the volunteers the reason why these behaviors are necessary from them. It is always easier to elicit a behavior from someone if that person knows why the behavior is important or is performed in a given way.

Some may say, however, that the change leader cannot tell volunteers where they can volunteer, that if a person wants to volunteer in a kindergarten, one must allow him or her to do so. This is not so. Remember that the principal or the change leader has the final say over who will be a volunteer in his or her school. With the additional emphasis on safety and security, in addition to new and higher standards, some people may not be acceptable as volunteers. If a place cannot be found for the skills of the volunteer, or if the volunteer simply is not acceptable, the change leader must say no to that volunteer, even if it is difficult to do so. Having the wrong volunteer in a program can have a negative impact upon that program and, more importantly, upon the students in that program.

As is easy to see, running a program for volunteers is not easy, but it can be a source of support. Volunteers can come into the schools and provide extra time. That time can be used to provide the opportunity for the teachers to teach smaller groups of students while the volunteers work with other students. It can be a time for students to build a nonthreatening relationship with an adult, and perhaps the student will talk about problems to that adult that he or she wouldn't speak about to a teacher. It can be time for a non-English-speaking student to get assistance from a native speaker if there is little ESL support in the school. These are all services that districts would like to have more of, yet cannot afford to pay for. The volunteerism is, in essence, "funding" the educational reform by providing time for additional services to the children.

Product Endorsement

Product endorsement is another way of securing funds for a school district, but it can be a very controversial subject. Corporations are willing to contribute large amounts of money to school districts that are willing to feature the corporation's logo or to endorse the corporation's products. While it is all well and good to receive additional money, the change leader needs to consider both sides of the question.

Clearly, additional money can help build stadia, can support programs, can assist with capital projects, and can be a boon to the school district. The other side of the question is more problematic and philosophical.

Is it appropriate to use students as an advertising or endorsement vehicle? If only "XYZ" soft drink is available in a school district, what are the repercussions? What if that soft drink company wants its logo on scoreboards and uniforms? Is that appropriate? How do the parents and the community feel about this? What is the extent to which the school district is willing to extend itself in courting these endorsements? Is the use of the money restricted? Looking to the future of the school district and product endorsement, how far is the school district willing to go in its search for additional funds? Does the school district want to endorse one soft drink, sneaker, or other consumer product over another? Should the district even be endorsing items? These are all questions that must be addressed.

REACHING BEYOND THE LOCAL COMMUNITY

Particularly in some districts where the schools are very rural or the area is economically disadvantaged, it may be difficult to raise additional funds from within the boundaries of the school district. In that case, the change leader must look to the areas that have a vested interest in the district's schools. Is there a community nearby where local residents go to work? Reach out to the businesses in that community. Is there a vendor from a different area with whom the district does a great deal of business? The change leader should seek support from that vendor.

Quality education is not merely a local concern. Everyone in the country should be concerned about improving the quality of education for the students who are our future. This will give the change leader leverage in asking for that help and assistance.

SUMMARY

There are methods that the change leader can use to raise funds or garner additional support for educational reform by tapping local resources. The success of these local methods of gathering support will depend on the compatibility of that method with the learning community. A method that is successful in one district will not be successful in another because of this link. A foundation may work well in a wealthy suburban district, but not in the inner city. A program of volunteers may work better in one community than in another.

Every chapter in this book has carried the plea that regardless of what the change leader chooses to do, that activity must support the reform of the school district. The change leader knows the students' needs and knows the community thoroughly; therefore he or she must match the skills and the knowledge of the community with the needs of the students. To do this is an investment of time on the part of the change leader, but it is well worth the effort because it is an investment in the reform of education for the students.

CHAPTER 7

Using Charter Schools to Fund Reform

It may appear that this chapter does not belong in a book on funding educational reform, yet the change leader must remember the ultimate goal of educational reform. That goal is to provide a better education with greater academic achievement for the students. Providing that improved education does not require that the change leader stay within the existing sphere of education, however. In fact, chapter 1 exhorted change leaders to think "outside the box" in funding and creating educational reform. Therefore charter schools should be viewed as just another alternative for helping that educational reform reach the students.

For the remainder of this chapter, schools will be referred to as either public schools or charter schools. The term *public schools* will be used to refer to those schools and districts that are a part of the existing educational system, run by the individual state. These are the schools that people have experienced in their own childhood and with which they are most familiar. The term *charter schools* will refer to those schools that have entered into an independent agreement with the state or other authorizing agency to provide educational services to the students of a particular state.

Before going on to the detailed ideas regarding the use of charter schools to fund educational reform, however, this chapter must begin with a series of caveats for all readers of this book. The goal is to ensure that the change leader is aware of both sides of the issue: how charter schools can be used to generate reform versus the obstacles that may impede that use.

Caveat Number One: Charter Schools Are Not a Panacea for All the Ills of Education. Clearly, ineffective practices have caused public schools to fail at producing well-educated students. If those very same ineffective practices are simply moved to a charter school venue, that charter school will fail in this also. For instance, in many public schools the favored teaching method is the lecture method, with the teacher standing in the front of the room talking to, or at, the students. If the very same method continues to be used in a charter school with no alteration of practice, no increase in achievement will be noted. Poor educational practices in charter schools will create low achievement among students, just as those poor educational practices have done in traditional public districts for many years.

The change leader must not assume that merely moving to a charter school scenario will make all the ineffective attributes of education disappear. As with other forms of funding for educational reform, the important issue for the change leader will be not that a particular form of funding and support has been chosen, but how that funding is used. If the choice of use of funding does not cause education to be delivered in a different way, the results will not change, either.

Caveat Number Two: Creating and Establishing a Charter School Is Hard Work. Many change leaders will have had the experience of moving into a newly constructed school building and can attest that a new school is a daunting challenge. It seems to be a truism that supplies will not arrive on time, there will be work left to be done on the building, and systems may not be in place. Yet a new school building will have the support of the school district office. A charter school will not generally have that kind of support. A charter school is more like its own miniature school district than merely another school in a district. The people who organize and who staff the charter school will need to be exceptionally dedicated to the task at hand. Establishing a charter school or moving to the charter school model will not be a quick fix without effort.

Caveat Number Three: This Is a Chapter for the Frustrated Change Leader. This chapter is for the person who has tried his or her best, over a long period of time, to infuse some of the ideas of reform into a school district or school system that does not want to change. This is not a chapter for someone who is merely annoyed at a school district, or someone who tried something once and perceived that no one wanted to listen, so is already willing to give up. This is a chapter for the change leader who feels that there is no going back to the existing educational system, and is willing to make the choice to leave it. If you have reached this level, please read on. This chapter will not give definitive answers, but it will raise questions that all change leaders must answer for themselves.

Once these caveats are accepted, the change leader can move on to explore the how and the why of using charter schools to fund reform.

WHAT IS A CHARTER SCHOOL?

The change leader will find a myriad of interpretations from various sources as to what a charter school really is. Naturally, those perceptions will vary widely.

Some people will see a charter school as an element of "the dark side," draining students and resources from the existing public school system. Others will see the charter school as a cure for all ills in education. Neither of those perceptions would be accurate. There are a few basic attributes that define a charter school. The first is that the charter school is a *school of choice*. This means that students do not attend the charter school solely by virtue of attendance area, like the attendance zones for schools and school districts. Instead the students choose to come to that charter school from whatever part of the authorized area in which the students live. A charter school may draw students from multiple public school districts as long as those districts are within the state that has authorized the charter. Naturally, distance will become a factor for parents' choice, but attendance is not limited by that.

Second, the charter school is established by a contract (the "charter") between the state government (or its designated oversight group) and the group of people establishing the charter school. This charter then specifies the parameters under which the school must operate: what grade levels are there, how many students are allowed, testing required, and so on.

Third, the charter is given for a finite period of time. Just because a charter school has been given a charter for three or five years does not mean that the charter school will be in existence forever. The charter must be renewed regularly, which means that the charter school is held accountable for achievement in a very direct way: low achievement can result in nonrenewal of the school's charter.

Fourth, a charter school is supported by tax dollars. Tuition is not charged as it is in a private school. Money to support the charter school will come in a per-pupil allocation from the individual state. The amounts and processes by which the charter school obtains these funds will vary in each state.

Simply put, a charter school is a public school of choice. All of the specific regulations for establishing and operating charter schools will vary from state to state, and all states will have different methods for application to establish a charter school, different funding mechanisms, and different methods for showing accountability to the state or authorizer. In all instances, though, the state regulates the charter school to ensure academic quality and fiscal stability.

In all charter schools there will be a board of directors of some sort that will provide governance. The change leader may be a part of this board, but is not a benevolent despot and will not have total individual control, so all of the attributes in chapter 1 will apply. The change leader will need to build trust with the public and the charter school constituencies, though there is a smaller direct audience. But there will be many others watching and judging. The change leader and the board of directors of the charter school will have to demonstrate integrity and accountability in both fiscal and instructional areas. The change leader will have to have focus for the school and will have to communicate well. A new area for the change leader may be the idea of marketing. To exist, the charter school needs to attract students. The change leader must communicate the vision and build trust in parents to encourage students to attend. Students in a charter school are not a captive audience as in the traditional public schools. A school of choice is where parents and students can "vote with their feet" by leaving the school to move to another or by staying with that school the next year. A charter school is not a way to avoid the difficult job of building trust.

PUBLIC OBJECTIONS TO CHARTER SCHOOLS

Since the concept of charter schools was first introduced, that very concept has been anathema to those already invested in the existing public school system. Just as some supporters of the existing educational system have seen private and parochial schools as a threat, charter schools are also considered to be a competitor. However, the change leader must realize that any alternative form of education that appears to vary from the established norm can expect to encounter resistance from the public school districts, so the change leader must be aware that the choice to follow the charter school route may be fraught with problems. Nonetheless, the most important consideration in the decision to go to a charter school must be the benefit to the student. If a change leader is seriously considering the move to charter status it is safe to assume that, in the years since *A Nation at Risk*, the public school district has not been able to deliver education more effectively to its students, nor has it been able to educate more students to higher levels. The change leader must therefore ask the question, Is a charter school going to serve the students of this district better than the existing schools?

Change leaders who are serious about beginning a charter school must understand the objections that will inevitably come their way as they seek to create the base for that formation of the charter school. This section of the chapter will delineate some of the more common objections, with information from both sides of the questions so that the change leader may be forewarned and prepared.

Objection Number One: Charter schools have been accused of draining resources from the existing public schools. In a way this is true, in that the public district may be required to provide transportation or other services to the students of the charter school in the same manner that it does for private school students. The charter school will also lower the amount of state aid received by the districts from which the charter school draws its students, but it is hardly a drain on those resources. Taking the nationwide average, charter schools receive about 80 percent of the per-pupil funding that a traditional public school does. Neither will the charter school necessarily receive all of the aids that will come to a public school district in a given state. For instance, a charter school may not receive help with the costs of building or renovating buildings.

Objection Number Two: Some educators in the existing public system will protest that charter schools are guilty of taking "the best and the brightest" students from the public schools. This has not been shown to be accurate. Charter schools receive, in many cases, a higher percentage of students who are "at risk" by virtue of poverty, insufficient academic skills, lack of English language facility, or other benchmarks. A commonsense assessment of the interactions in schools will confirm this. By and large, if parents are satisfied with a district public school, they will not wish to take their children from the district school where they are successful nor from the company of all of their friends. If a parent is frustrated, however, he or she is *more* likely to take his or her child from an existing public school and move that child to a charter school. The reasons why a parent may be frustrated all relate to a lack of success for the child in the public school: the student is not progressing in his or her achievement. Therefore, since the parents who are dissatisfied with district schools are the parents of the students who are failing in the existing system, the students who are likely to move to a charter school will be the students with some type of learning difficulty.

Objection Number Three: Another cry will be that the change leader is abandoning the system of public education, that the change leader should be "working from the inside," using his or her talents to better the students' education in the public district. This chapter assumes that the change leader will have tried his or her best to do that very thing before leaving the public school district. Educators are loyal to public education, but there may come a point where the change leader must try another avenue to implement reform. If a change leader has worked for a number of years to reform education and has not been satisfied with the results, the plea that he or she should remain, working even harder or even longer in a place where there has been no change, is minimizing the value of that change leader's previous efforts.

Objection Number Four: Some people, both within and outside of the existing educational system, will claim that charter schools will be the death of the public educational system, and that such a revered institution as public schools must be maintained and preserved. This alleged wholesale abandonment of public schools has not materialized since charter school legislation came into being in the early 1990s. Instead, parents have been given a choice of where and how to have their children educated. Some parents have exercised that choice.

While the objections that the change leader will hear are not as serious as they seem to be when considered factually, the change leader must keep in mind that he or she will be fighting against firmly held perceptions in the arena of public opinion as the charter school is applied for and as it begins. During the application process and all during operation, both the opponents and the proponents of the school will watch the charter school very closely. Any failure on the part of one charter school will be automatically generalized to apply to all charter schools; therefore the change leader and the establishing group must ensure that everything in the charter school, from instruction to finance, is done as well as possible.

A committed group is essential in starting a charter school within an existing school district because the change leader cannot expect a great deal of help from the local school district. The change leader must well understand that a charter school opening in a given school district may be a threat to that school district. The opening of a charter school will be perceived as a very public statement that the district in which the charter school resides has failed in its job of educating students, and the local school district may not take kindly to that implication. The change leader may expect some resistance from the local school district, or perhaps even hostility. The superintendent may be insulted. The board of education may be insulted. At the very least, be assured that everyone in the community will be watching very closely.

BEFORE LEAVING THE EXISTING EDUCATIONAL SYSTEM

Before leaving the public school district and in order to obviate the objection, erroneous as it may be, that the change leader has abandoned public education, the change leader must be sure that he or she has exhausted all of the possibilities of reform within the school district. This means that the change leader must have the answers to the following questions, for himself or herself if not to share with others.

- Has the problem or problems that created the need for reform in the district been clearly identified? This does not mean identified in a general way like "Math scores in the eighth grade are low." This means identified in terms of being able to determine specific needs like "Students in the eighth grade are not able to correctly solve for an unknown in algebraic equations" or "Students on the fourth grade reading test are not able to draw information from a written article or paragraph." In a quest to reform, a district should have identified a number of these problems or skill deficiencies. Have these been identified yet? Has the district addressed the identified problem(s) adequately, or has only lip service been given to reform? Is there a lot of talking and a lot of committee work taking place, but no change in the classrooms? Is the school district still denying that there is a problem that needs to be reformed? If the implementation has started, where is the implementation on the timeline?

- Has a tentative method for establishing the reform been selected? Has the district decided what it is going to do to remedy the problems that have been identified? In order to decide this, the district will have had to do analyses of what may be causing the problem(s) to occur. Has a new textbook been selected, or a new curriculum written? Have teachers been trained in a new method if one is needed? What behavior or outcome will show if the reform has been a success?

- If the implementation phase of the reform is complete, how long has the complete reform been in place? The change leader must give the reform an opportunity to demonstrate a difference before saying that it isn't effective. Research says that a timeline of three to five years is necessary to see proof of different outcomes for students, and literature on change tells us that it takes five years for a change to become institutionalized. Change is not a quick fix.

- Have teacher behaviors changed? Are teachers doing anything differently? Do the teachers believe the reform will work, or are they only "going through the motions"?

- Has administrative behavior changed? If teachers are being expected to do things differently, is that being reflected in their yearly evaluations? Do the administrators believe the reform will work, or are they only "going through the motions"?

- Are student outcomes different? Has there been any change in the test scores or in the items that have been identified as benchmarks?

- What is the student reaction to the reform? The change leader should ask the older students. Are things being taught differently? Are things easier to understand?

- Has the reform been communicated well? For instance, if the reform is in math, are the math teachers the only ones who know about it, or can the Spanish teachers talk about what the reform is also? Is that reform the focus of everyone's work, or of only a few?
- Does the superintendent support the reform? Does the board of education support the reform? The change leader must answer these questions based on actions since if the reform is supported, then actions will reflect that support.
- Does the community support the reform? Are the members of the PTA able to talk about the reform? Have they been given periodic updates? Do they know what behaviors to look for in order to judge the efficacy of the reform?
- Is anything being measured to indicate success or failure? What is being measured? Is it a valid measure of the results of the reform?
- Have the necessary qualities of integrity and accountability been used to create trust of the school district within the public?
- Is decision making site-based or handed down from the central office level?

If the answers to any of these questions indicate that there is more that a change leader can do, then the change leader has a choice of remaining with the existing educational system to rectify what has yet to be done *or* choosing to move to a charter school. And the answers to the questions will provide a road map for the change leader if he or she goes ahead to establish a charter school.

HOW CAN A CHARTER SCHOOL FUND REFORM?

Obviously, the simple establishment of a charter school cannot provide additional money as a grant or other method of funding would be able to do. What a charter school can do, however, is to fund reform by forcing a reallocation of resources. The introduction to this book referred to *A Nation at Risk* and how education has not substantively changed in many areas despite a more than adequate amount of time to show results. In addition to adequate time, the amount of money that federal, state, and local governments have spent on education has increased.

Thus, the increased spending with no demonstrable results showing increased achievement indicates that these increased resources have not been used in different ways. Rather, these resources have been used to support the same established ways of delivering education, despite the governmental avowal that change is needed. A charter school can at least reallocate a part of those resources and direct even that small amount of the existing resources to reform.

This is where the concept of focus becomes very important. Because charter schools are freed from some of the constraints of educational regulations and of educational traditions, a charter school may be an opportunity to fund reform by reallocating time and effort. As an example, a charter school may have the freedom to reallocate time by creating a longer school day or year, where the same efforts in a traditional public school would probably have to be paid for by use of overtime or other ways of extending services beyond the school day, or by hiring additional people to provide services within the school day. A state may also allow freedom from some lesser mandates that apply to public schools, such as two periods of physical education per week. Having only one period of physical education for each class each week might allow the charter school to use that time for a different purpose.

The group that establishes the charter school must consider the use of the extra time. Will it be additional academic time? Will the charter school have a theme, like music or technology, for which the additional time could be used? The charter school can then use the expanded time that it has in a wiser manner, concentrating on the efforts of reform to increase student achievement or providing an enriched curriculum to increase student achievement. By using time in a different way, the change leader is, in essence, funding reform. The change leader must remember that funding is not always done with money alone.

STARTING A CHARTER SCHOOL IS NOT AS EASY AS IT SEEMS

The change leader who opts to open a charter school can be a member of the community or can be a sitting superintendent, but for neither change leader will the establishment of the charter school be an easy one. There are "hoops" that the change leader will have to negotiate his or her way through in the process of establishing a charter school. Some states have a massive application process, or even a "defense" of the proposed charter before a judging panel. Funds to start the charter school may not be as much as hoped. All of the skills in chapter 1 that are required of a change leader in a school district will be required of a change leader starting a charter school.

The change leader must build trust among the prospective constituencies of the charter school that he or she has the best interests of the students at heart. The *integrity* of the process must be maintained. Groups joining in the creation of a charter school are looking for a leader, a "savior" perhaps, but someone who will make a difference in education. The change leader will have to be very careful that promises are not made that cannot be kept. Vague or "pie in the sky"-type assurances that don't materialize will be the death of the change leader's support.

Fiscal *accountability* is paramount. Records for moneys that are contributed for the creation and start-up of the charter school must be zealously maintained. The least intimation of fiscal wrongdoing can be fatal to the start-up. Moneys must be spent effectively, too. The change leader cannot, for instance, start the spending for the charter school with a well-equipped office for the principal, or hire the relatives of members of the establishing group without a proper bidding process.

The change leader should note that in some states there is a dismal record of charter schools failing. In few of these instances is the academic failure of these schools cited. Rather, the charter schools failed to adequately monitor the noninstructional tasks of school operation, and foremost among these are the financial tasks that the charter school must complete.

A primary concern of the change leader, naturally, will be the instructional *focus* of the charter school. A charter school must do things differently from the existing educational system if different outcomes are sought, and, patently, they are. Before starting a charter school the change leader is going to have to ask himself or herself questions about how education is going to be delivered, and not merely in terms of what book will be used for a certain class. The change leader will need to think through teaching methods, choosing curricula, which materials to use, and all the areas that touch the students. It is a massive undertaking.

Will the charter school simply take the curricula that are in use in the local public schools? Why? Will new curricula be developed? By whom? Will the new curricula meet the state standards? Will there be a class size limit? What grades will be included in the charter school? The change leader will also need to be familiar with the laws and regulations governing the charter school and what can or cannot be done within those parameters.

The change leader will also have to focus on and provide for all of the concerns that the public district's central office provides that are virtually invisible to a traditional school building site. The largest of these is the concern about the actual site itself. Charter schools may not get state funding for capital expenses—the money needed to build or renovate a building. That has to be sought through other avenues. Once the building is purchased, who will clean and maintain it? The building will need insurances, inspections, and will have to be maintained to meet building codes. Who will be responsible for ensuring that? There are other centrally organized services that will need to be provided. Will there be computer support? Will free and reduced price meals be available? Who will transport the students? How will people get their paychecks? Who will hire and fire personnel? Who will develop and monitor the budget? Who will fill out applications for entitlement grants and any competitive grants being sought? There are numerous areas that support student achievement by supporting the organization and operation of the school that the change leader will need to address.

Communication skills will be paramount as the change leader shares the vision of providing for reform through the use of a charter school. Participation of community groups is also required as a charter moves through the application process. The change leader will have to build the base of support among all of the founding and potential groups in the district.

Establishing a charter school is not a way to avoid the difficult tasks of building trust through integrity, accountability, maintaining focus, and communication. Chapter 1 referred also to *decentralized decision making* and "*outside the box*" thinking. Starting a charter school can be the epitome of those skills, also.

TYPES OF CHARTER SCHOOLS

Another dilemma that the change leader will have to face is that of choosing the model of charter school that is needed. For this purpose there are basically three models of charter schools: *independent*, where a community group organizes and runs a charter school on its own with the only assistance coming from state and other charter school groups, and two *contracted* models where a community group or a district hires a charter school management company to assist it with the management of the charter school in a variety of ways. This section of the chapter will give the pros and cons of each type of charter school to the change leader.

Independent Charter School. An individual or a group may decide to open a charter school on its own. This can be very time intensive for those individuals. Not only will the establishing group need to take the charter school through the application process, but the establishing group will need to decide all of the instructional and operational issues mentioned previously in this chapter. The group must remember that while some of these issues seem small, like deciding how the building will be cleaned, these issues impact the students in the day-to-day operations of the school.

Contracted Charter School with Management of Building Services Only. In this first contracted model, a charter school management company is hired to take over the management of a building or a district, in much the same way that transportation or cafeteria services are contracted out in a school district. This may assist the charter school with some of the tasks that the creators of the charter school may not wish, or have the expertise, to address, that is, state filings, accounting, benefits, payroll, and so on. The management company does not address academics or instruction.

If engaging an educational management company, the change leader should check to ensure precisely what services are included. A charter school is more similar to a small school district than it is to an individual school building within a school district. All of the complexities of operating a total school district are present in a charter school. The establishing group of the charter school will be responsible for ensuring that all of those complexities are provided for.

Contracted Charter School with Management of Building Services and Curriculum. The second contracted model includes academic management. The charter school management company will supervise all the functions of the school, both operational and instructional. The charter school management company may bring a developed curriculum into the school as well as providing the "central office services" that are provided under a management-only model. The management company will also provide supervision and implementation of the instructional portion of the school operations.

If considering this model of charter school, the change leader must be very aware of the needs of the students. While it may be a great deal easier to simply accept a complete curriculum, the change leader must look at the needs of the school. Does the management company's curriculum address the educational weaknesses that have been identified in the vision for the charter school? For instance, if the educational weakness identified is math, make sure the math curriculum is strong. If not, do not accept that management company's planned curriculum. Be sure to use the money allocated to the charter school, whether state, federal, local, or private, to support the program that will work for the students.

The change leader must also be sure that the methods of teaching and educating that the educational management company supports are congruent with the beliefs of the charter school. There are different curricula associated with different management companies, and those differing curricula may require differing instructional techniques. The establishing group must ask questions such as: What is the philosophy of instruction in the vision of the proposed charter school? Does the charter school believe in the philosophy of direct instruction or some other method? Does the charter school want technology integrated across the curriculum? Does the management company's curriculum address state standards? The group establishing the charter school must choose wisely for the benefit of the students.

The change leader and the establishing charter school group need to consider the cost aspect of contracting also. As in the rest of the world, a charter school will not "get something for nothing." In both models (management of building services only or management of instruction as well as building services) the establishing group will have to sign a management contract stating that the charter school will pay a fee for these management services. Each educational management company has a different structure for these fees. Contracting for someone else to administer the charter school will cost money, but may allow the change leader to focus more on instructional issues than on noninstructional issues. A fully developed curriculum that meets the needs of the students and will bring higher achievement is worth a great deal. The change leader must consider these questions.

THE CHARTER SCHOOL AS A PART OF AN EXISTING SCHOOL DISTRICT

Not only can a community group contract with a charter school company, but a district may contract for a charter school under the auspices of that district, or, in some cases, a district may charter the entire district. The change leader must be aware that the concept of using a charter school within an existing district is a very controversial idea. Some people may see it as a district's admission of failure. The change leader may see it as an opportunity to provide choice for parents and their children.

The No Child Left Behind Act may be paving the way for alternative schooling like this by mandating choice if a school or district is failing. Would it be better for a school district to have to send students and funds to other districts, or would it be more effective to establish that choice within the district? The difference between the district schools and the charter school would have to be that the charter school would educate students in a profoundly different way from the existing school district. That would be the only way to provide in-district choice under No Child Left Behind.

There are some potential problems inherent in this approach to reform. A charter school within a district or a totally chartered district may have difficulties in delivering education differently to the students if the management company also has to work within the existing confines of the established district. Will the management company be required to assume all existing contracts in the building, including teachers, administrators, support staff, contractors, and so forth? Or can modifications be made to existing labor contracts? Will existing district practices, policies, and procedures still apply to that building, or can the chartered portion of the district develop its own? There may be no appreciable change in achievement if the curricula in the charter school portion of the district are the exact same curricula in use in the remainder of the district.

There is a large number of questions that the change leader must answer.

SUMMARY

A charter school is a public school of choice.

However, using a charter school to fund reform is far too complex an issue to be dealt with in one chapter of a book. The goal here is to ensure that the change leader is aware of the fact that the opening of a charter school is an option that is available.

Districts or change leaders should never opt for a charter school because they think it is a cheaper way to deliver education. The only criterion should be whether or not the charter school provides an opportunity for a better education. The goal of the change leader is to increase achievement of the students, so the only reason for a change leader to move to a charter school is to increase that achievement.

Clearly education is going through a time when we, as educators, have to start thinking about delivering education in vastly different ways: different schedules, different requirements leading to achievement, different funding approaches, different ideas. But the primary consideration is always the same: What will these new approaches to thinking about education do for the achievement of the students?

CHAPTER 8

Going Forward from Here:
Actions for the Change Leader

As the change leader has been able to see throughout this book, educational reform, and the funding of such, is much more than just an issue of paying the bills. In its most basic terms educational reform can be summarized in two simple strictures: *Choose the most effective programs on which to spend educational reform money* and *Be completely ethical and correct in the processes that are used in spending public money.*

CHAPTER 1

In chapter 1 this book talked about the most important factor in spending public money of any kind: the establishment and maintenance of trust. If a change leader does nothing else, it is necessary for him or her to build trust with the public of the school district. The change leader is asking the constituencies of the school district to entrust the district with not only the improvement of education for the children and the future, but with the use of the money that the public has contributed, albeit sometimes unwillingly, for that purpose. It sometimes appears that no other governmental entity is concerned with building this trust. Therefore the change leader must set himself or herself and his or her district apart in this.

The change leader may find different reactions from members of the public when establishing what is perceived to be a different style or pattern than is expected from a governmental entity. Some members of the public will be skeptical, or even openly incredulous. They have had the experience of promises that representatives of a governmental agency have made, but never kept. Some members of the public may simply ignore the attempts of the change leader to establish that different style because they do not believe that change can make a difference. On the whole, however, the members of the public who are concerned about the quality of education in the district and about the effective use of district money will embrace the change leader's steps toward establishment of trust.

The constituencies of a school district are looking for a person who will lead them in honesty and in integrity. Members of tax PAC lobby groups will welcome the accountability. Parents, particularly, will welcome the focus on educational quality. All constituencies of the school district will welcome their inclusion in district decision making as the change leader opens decisions up to decentralized processes. All constituencies will also welcome open and honest communication. A change leader could even become a kind of hero or cult figure in the community as the person who opened the educational process of the school district to the scrutiny and knowledge of the public.

While the change leader certainly does not have to go to the extreme lengths of becoming a community hero, any movement in the direction of clarifying issues and showing accountability will be viewed as a positive step in the eyes of the school district's public. However, full implementation of all of the steps in chapter 1—integrity, accountability, focus, decentralized decision making, and communication—will always reap the greatest reward for the change leader. This book has tried to always focus on practical, usable information. Therefore, here are some behaviors that the change leader can begin with tomorrow in his or her district:

Integrity. The change leader should never say one thing, but do another. The behaviors of the change leader should reflect the beliefs of the change leader.

The change leader must never make a promise that he or she cannot keep. If information is promised to a board member, a teacher, or a taxpayer by a certain date, the change leader must do everything possible to ensure that the information is received in a timely manner.

If the change leader cannot meet a deadline or fulfill a promise, an explanation must be given. Preferably this should be done well in advance of the deadline, so that it doesn't look like an afterthought.

If the change leader does not know an answer, he or she must acknowledge that. The change leader can always reply to a person with accurate information at a later date, but it is impossible to fully retract inaccurate words spoken in haste.

The change leader should never ask a staff member to do something that the change leader is unwilling to do himself or herself. For instance, if a change leader wants teachers to eat lunch with students, the change leader should make sure that he or she is present there sometimes, also. If the change leader wants all staff to be at work on time, the change leader should be on time as an example before he or she requires that of others.

Do not fall into the trap of educational arrogance. Educators can and should learn from others.

Accountability. The change leader must not only spend public money effectively, but the change leader must ensure that the money is spent on programs that are effective in furthering the reform.

The change leader must follow precisely all laws and regulations guiding the use of public money.

In addition, it is imperative that accurate records be maintained. These records must be open to public scrutiny (they are public information in any case). Members of the public can have helpful suggestions.

The change leader must report regularly on financial matters in a clear, easy-to-understand format.

Focus. The change leader must keep the students at the center of all conversations and decisions. Make sure that everything is discussed with the consideration of how it will benefit the students.

The change leader must share information on the reform. He or she can start by simply talking about the reform at every opportunity, in an informal conversation, in a discussion group, or in a faculty meeting. The change leader must share the vision of reform with others.

The change leader must choose programs that have been proved to be effective in bringing about the desired reform in a district that is demographically similar to the change leader's school district. The imperative to change is urgent; do not squander precious time on unproven programs.

Decentralized Decision Making. The change leader must ask staff for input. The people who are closest to the issue, in this case, reform, have the best ideas for its implementation.

Don't limit the change leader's quest for input to only those who are acknowledged experts in a question. The custodian or cafeteria worker may have a good idea that relates to the reform. No one should be excluded in the change leader's quest to think outside the box.

Communication. Above all, the change leader must be honest.

The change leader must not use educational jargon.

The change leader must not "spin" information, even though that is acceptable in many other areas of the culture.

The change leader must listen to what people have to say. It is the best way to learn, as well as to enhance credibility.

Some of these behaviors can begin immediately. Others require more preparation, but can still be implemented soon. The most important thing is for the change leader to take a step forward tomorrow morning.

CHAPTER 2

A change leader who has the most accurate data for his or her school district can use state aid formulas to their maximum potential. This is the first step that a change leader can undertake in ensuring that the greatest amount of money from state aid is made available to the school district. Remember that when more money is available overall, more money can be focused on the reform of the district.

What can the change leader do tomorrow? Start setting up processes that will result in the most accurate data. If the district already has processes, check to make sure that the data is accurate. Existing processes may have to be modified. The change leader will have to work with the technology department and all principals to ensure operation of these processes.

The change leader can go to the school district business administrator to ask for some tutoring in educational finance.

The change leader might even consider becoming involved in the groups that seek to modify state aid formulas. Since most state aid formulas are currently subject to political negotiations, the change leader will want to work toward establishing in his or her state a state aid formula that will respond to needs; the needs that the formula responds to should include the needs of the students as well as the needs of the school district. Recognition that some areas of a state may be more expensive to operate in and recognition that some students may be more costly to educate should both be a part of a modified state aid formula. There are national groups, as well as statewide and local groups, where the change leader could work on this issue.

CHAPTER 3

Clearly, the change leader is not able to increase the amount of money that is given in federal entitlement grants without the help of others. Changing the amount of money given in these grants is a lobbying effort that includes educators and legislators from across the country. The change leader can become a part of that.

However, since increasing the amount of money for an individual district is not under the control of the change leader alone, the next best strategy for the change leader to take is to make sure that the use of the federal entitlement money is focused as much as possible on the implementation of the district's reform initiative. Federal grants in many districts have been the funding source for programs that "have always been there" because the funds are separate from the district's general operating funds. The change leader has an opportunity in this instance to take that federal money and apply it to programs that will assist the programs in the district's general operating funds rather than exist in parallel with those programs.

The change leader needs to ensure that he or she is cognizant of all of the guidelines of No Child Left Behind, and of the latest interpretations of those guidelines. As No Child Left Behind endures through the year, the change leader must also be aware of modifications that are made to that law on a yearly basis. The change leader may even wish to become involved with groups that are studying NCLB or that are lobbying the government for changes. Many of the provisions can be seen as onerous to some school districts. It is the right of those districts in a democracy to lobby for changes. The change leader should remember, however, that the intent of NCLB may be the same as that of the change leader: reform of education.

CHAPTER 4

The property taxes that support education in a community are always problematic for the educators in that school district. Taxpayers can identify much more closely with the local school district than they can with a distant state or federal government.

The change leader should begin by learning about tax issues in the community. What are the tax groups involved? What are the objections? How valid are the objections? Then, using all of the skills delineated in chapter 1, the change leader must set out to educate his or her public on the issues of property taxation. In fact, while these skills are important in every instance of financing reform, in no area are those skills more important than in dealing with issues of local property taxes.

In the area of property taxes, accountability is probably the most important trait to learn and to communicate. Ethical use of money and frequent reporting of financial status will be imperative if the change leader is to build trust in this area.

CHAPTER 5

Competitive grants are very different from the federal entitlement grants that the change leader will deal with. A competitive grant is not a guaranteed revenue, where state and federal aid can be predicted, usually, with a much higher degree of accuracy. Even the reception of a competitive grant by a school district cannot be guaranteed, so the change leader should never depend upon competitive grants for funds for support of educational reform.

The money from competitive grants can, however, be viewed as a pleasant addition to the funding of educational reform in the district. If a district can secure money from a competitive grant, then even more money than was planned can be directed to reform, making the reform stronger, and perhaps helping implement phases sooner.

There are a number of methods that the change leader can use to secure a competitive grant. The change leader can write the competitive grant himself or herself. In this case the change leader should be sure to adhere to the suggestions in chapter 5. The school district can hire a grant writer whose responsibility is to seek grants for the school district. Or the district can contract grant-writing services to a consultant. In any case, additional money can be found to support the reform of the school district.

CHAPTER 6

Local sources of funds may not generate the amount of money that comes from the governmental sources, but there are other aspects that may prove positive to the implementation of reform. Working with local groups can increase community involvement in the schools and in the reform plan, also hopefully increasing the community "buy-in" or ownership of the school programs and reform. For this reason alone the change leader may wish to approach local funding sources.

Partnerships, fund-raising, and volunteerism can help community members feel that they are contributing to the health as well as the wealth of the school district. Remember that goodwill and a feeling of ownership can go a long way in supporting the trust that the change leader is building within the public toward the school district.

The step of communication, step 5, will be very important here. The change leader may have to bring together disparate groups who may have the same goals, but different methods for achieving them.

CHAPTER 7

In the event that a change leader is totally frustrated within the existing educational system, he or she may take the drastic step of turning the school district over to a charter school management company in its totality, or of establishing a charter school option under the auspices of the school district. The change leader should be aware that this is a very controversial concept, and it cannot be accomplished quickly.

SUMMARY

This book has set out some ideas for the steps that a change leader can take to improve the funding of educational reform, and to find additional moneys to support educational reform. These steps may not be easy solutions. Change takes time and effort to be implemented. It is also possible that the existing educational bureaucracy may not appreciate change for the sake of reform. Nonetheless, the only consideration that should matter to the change leader is the benefit of the reform to the students of the school district. Benefit to the students makes worthwhile the time and the effort invested in reforming education.

Resources

No change leader can possibly know everything about change, about leadership, or about educational finance. For that reason this section will list resources that have been used in the formation of the philosophies underlying this book, and to which the change leader can refer should he or she wish to delve into a particular subject on a deeper level.

Over the years a myriad of books and articles have been written to assist the change leader in learning about change and educational finance. Therefore, this cannot be a complete list. The change leader should feel free to seek as many different points of view as possible. The strength of the change leader lies in selecting the skills that will work in a given situation.

Experts in the day-to-day application of the ideas expressed in this book who have assisted in its preparation should also be acknowledged. These practitioners are:

Brandon Gordon
Executive Director
Midstate School Finance Consortium
6390 Fly Road
East Syracuse, NY 13057

Shannon Metcalf, Ph.D.
Coordinator of Federal Programs
Mosaica Education, Inc.
1013 Centre Road
Wilmington, Delaware 19805

Ray Sanchez
Funded Programs Coordinator
Ossining Union Free School District
190 Croton Avenue
Ossining, New York 10562

BIBLIOGRAPHY

Abowitz, K. K. 2002. From public education to educational publics. *Clearing House* 76 (1): 34–38.

Achilles, C. M., and K. B. Ruskin. 1995. *Grant writing, fundraising, & partnerships: Strategies that work.* Newbury Park, CA: Sage.

Anderson, A. 1996. *Ethics for fundraisers.* Bloomington: Indiana University Press.

Astuto, T. A., D. L. Clark, A. Read, K. McGree, L. deKoven, and P. Fernandez. 1994. *Roots of reform: Challenging the assumptions that control change in education.* Bloomington, IN: Phi Delta Kappa Educational Foundation.

Bauer, D. G. 1994. *The principal's guide to winning grants.* New York: Scholastic.

———. 1999. *The teacher's guide to winning grants.* San Francisco: Jossey-Bass.

Brown, L. G., and M. J. Brown. 2001. *De-mystifying grant seeking: What you really need to do to get grants.* San Francisco: Jossey-Bass.

Browning, B. A. *Grant writing for dummies.* 2001. New York: Hungry Minds.

Carlson, M., and the Alliance for Non-Profit Management. 2002. *Winning grants step by step.* San Francisco: Jossey-Bass.

Ciconte, B. L., B. K. Ciconte, and J. G. Jacob. 2003. *Fundraising basics: A complete guide.* Boston: Jones & Bartlett.

Clark, D. M. 1992. Business–education partnerships. *Resources in Education* 27 (3).

Clarke, C. A. 2001. *Storytelling for grant seekers: The guide to creative non-profit fundraising.* San Francisco: Jossey-Bass.

DuBrin, A. J. 1998. *The complete idiot's guide to leadership.* New York: Alpha Books, John A. Woods, CWL Publishing Enterprises.

Finn, C. E., Jr., and L. A. Bierlein. 1996. Finding the right fit. *Brookings Review* 14 (3): 18–21.

Fusarelli, L. D. 2002. Charter schools implications for teachers and administrators. *Clearing House* 76 (1): 20–24.

Jackson, J., J. C. Jackson, and E. Beier. 2003. *Beyond the bake sale: The ultimate school fundraising book.* New York: St. Martin's Press.

Jasso, G. 1996. *Finding corporate resources*. Newbury Park, CA: Sage.

Karsh, E., and A. S. Fox. 2003. *The only grant-writing book you'll ever need*. New York: Carroll & Graf.

Lockwood, A.T., and M. Bryans. 2002. Charter districts. *School Administrator* 59 (6): 12–13, 15–17.

New, C. C., and J. A. Quick. 1998. *Grant seekers' tool kit*. New York: John Wiley & Sons.

Odden, A., and S. Archibald. 2001. *Reallocating resources: How to boost student achievement without asking for more*. Thousand Oaks, CA: Corwin.

Odden, A., and C. Busch. 1998. *Financing schools for high performance: Strategies for improving the use of educational resources*. San Francisco: Jossey-Bass.

Senge, P. M. 1990. *The fifth discipline*. New York: Doubleday.

———. 2000. *Schools that learn*. New York: Doubleday.

Sergiovanni, T. J. 1990. *Value-added leadership*. New York: Harcourt Brace Jovanovich.

Tremore, J., and N. B. Smith. 2003. *The everything grant writing book: Create the perfect proposal to raise the funds you need*. Avon, MA: Adams Media.

Warden, C., and D. Lauber. 1998. *School based budgeting: Your money, your business*. Chicago: Cross City Campaign for Urban School Reform.

Index

Note: Italic numerals indicate tables.

About the Author

Agnes Gilman Case has extensive experience as an educator beginning in 1978, serving first as a reading teacher and then as a Spanish teacher, with experience in an urban school district as well as in a rural area. Dr. Case has always been an advocate of educational reform, writing new curricula, serving on committees, and volunteering to be a part of new and innovative programs in the school district.

In 1993 Dr. Case took her efforts and desire to make education more effective into the school district business office by becoming certified as a school business administrator. From that office she sought to apply the principles of chapter 1 in focusing the efforts of reform in the school district. Dr. Case has trained numerous administrators in the concepts of educational finance that they need and has implemented and supported decentralized decision making. She has also been a resource for community groups and board members seeking to understand the ramifications of financial decisions in their district.

In 2003 Dr. Case moved to a different area of educational reform and began work with an educational management company.

Dr. Case holds a B.S. in psychology, an M.S. in reading education, a certificate of advanced study in school business administration, and an Ed.D. in educational administration.